Build Green ...
Make Green ...
Save Green ...

A practical guide for
environmentally-responsible home building

Adam D. Bearup

Edited by: Lyn Cryderman
Cover Design by: Barb Zimmerman
Book Illustrated by: Barb Zimmerman
Additional Illustrations by: Stephanie Bearup
Photo Credits: Hybrid Homes, LLC

For additional information or to contact the author,
visit: www.adambearup.com

DEDICATION

This book is dedicated to those who wonder
what's over the next hill.

ACKNOWLEDGEMENTS

I would like to thank my parents who have always supported my passions and have made it possible for me to live life on the road for so many years as I compiled the information for this book. My parents have known when to step back and let me push the limits of everything that I have done or built. That means many times that they had to see me cry, crash and burn, and scrape things up to feed myself and my dog Jagger, all while I demanded that they *not* help me. They would literally help wipe the dust off of my back, pick me up, and say "don't give up, keep going, it's worth it." I love you Dad, Mom and Gerard, for without your help, none of this would have been possible.

I would also like to thank my wife Stephanie and her family for the love and support they give me. Stephanie you constantly amaze me with your love and support!

I would like to thank all of those homeowners who took a chance on having us build their houses to prove that we could achieve the results that we all knew that we could achieve. The information that I gathered for this book was gathered while building their homes.

Finally, I would like to thank all of those people who helped me by letting me sleep on their couch while I lived life on the road and/or helped me work through different life lessons. All of you helped me in your own way, and I will never forget it.

TABLE OF CONTENTS

FOREWORD

I began my working life as a carpenter, and much later became a doctor. I used to joke that the difference between carpentry and medicine is that medicine is easier—there's no such thing as a board stretcher.

Since then, my life has taken many unexpected turns, and now I work full-time on helping people become better stewards of the planet. Along the way, I've built two passive solar homes for my family and advised colleges on energy efficient housing. I write books on the subject and have spoken with hundreds of groups across the country about conserving resources. But most importantly, I try to walk the talk.

About a decade ago, I started looking for ways to better aligning my beliefs with my actions. My wife and I decided we did not need to live in a large home that used so much energy, so we sold it and built a house with the same exact footprint as our old garage—getting rid of about half our possessions along the way. Over the course of a couple of years, we completely changed the way we live—cutting back our fossil fuel use by more than two-thirds and our trash production by nine-tenths.

You might think that all these changes made our lives more difficult, but the reverse happened. Living out our theology has made our lives much better. We have fewer "things" to worry about, which allows us to enjoy life more.

So when I learned what Adam Bearup was trying to do in the

housing industry, I was overjoyed. Every time he builds a house that uses significantly less energy than conventional homes, he is helping take care of the earth. And by sharing what he has learned about environmentally-responsible construction techniques, he is helping others care for the planet as well.

It would be easy to look at all that is being done to harm the planet and feel as if the situation is hopeless—that little things like adding more insulation to our homes, switching to energy-efficient lighting, or recycling our trash will never solve the huge environmental issues we face. Whenever I feel discouraged, I remember Mother Teresa's answer to a similar question about how mankind could possibly solve the problem of global poverty: "One person at a time."

And that's what Adam Bearup is doing—contributing to a healthier environment, one house at a time. If you read this book and decide to have a house built that uses these environmentally-responsible construction methods, you will be joining a growing movement of people who love the planet enough to care for it as if it were a rare and beautiful gift given by a loving Creator.

> Matthew Sleeth, M.D.
> Executive Director of
> Blessed Earth, and author of
> *Serve God, Save the Planet*

For more energy-saving ideas, visit www.blessedearth.org

INTRODUCTION

First off, I want to thank you for reading this book!

It will not take you very long to find out that this book contains more than just a guide to building environmentally-responsible homes. When I was researching how to write a book, I was told over and over again to find an editor to help assemble the pages and pages of text. An editor takes the author's writings and helps to mold it into a collection of words than not only makes sense, but also, tells the entire story that the author is trying to tell. Thank you to Lyn Cryderman who edited this book.

Lyn has helped me to develop the story of why I wanted to build these environmentally-responsible projects, not just how we built them. Lyn's advice helped me to create a story and not just a text book. You are about to experience life as I experienced it, on the bleeding edge of technology! You will want to know what happened next and why I didn't quit, even when faced with what seemed like un-conquerable obstacles. Lyn helped me to create a book that makes you feel like you are sitting next to me in a coffee shop listening to the story.

Throughout this book, you will find "callouts." These callouts will be in the form of boxes with text in them. The text in these boxes is placed close to where they appear in the book. The idea of the callout boxes is for you to post the text you see in those boxes onto your social media pages, i.e. Facebook, Twitter, (or anything else that may exist when you read this book.) My hopes are that you will help me to introduce your friends to ideas that will help to improve the environment. By doing this, you will help me to spread the word that we CAN improve the environment around us. Person by person, friend by friend, we can have a positive effect!

Here is how it works

First, read this book by your computer, smart phone, tablet, or any other device that may be available when you read this book. As you encounter a callout box, pause your reading of the book, read what is in the box and then post what is mentioned in the text box to your social media account. **By doing this, you can help me to improve the environment!** The goal is for you to spark a conversation on your page which will ultimately lead your friends to understanding that there are simple ways to improve the environment they live in and around. As I can, I will chime in on your posts to create conversations and to keep people thinking out of the box.

You do not have to live on the road with me to make a difference. You can use your social media pages to be part of an environmental movement that is growing by the day! While you post these different passages, you should feel like you are part of a large group of people who care, who want to help. We, as a group, can let our friends know that we care about them and the environment.

Get ready for a fun, entertaining book that will keep you thinking outside the box. Once you read this book, please let someone you know read it, or better yet, buy them a copy and suggest they use the social media route to helping their friends to improve their environment!

To contact me, email me at: **hybridhomeguy@gmail.com** and/or visit **www.adambearup.com**.

Yours very truly,

Adam D. Bearup

1 TRYING TO CHANGE AN INDUSTRY

It all started with a call from my cousin Jim.

"How come no one is paying attention to all your talk about the need to build energy-efficient homes?" he asked.

Good question.

And he was right—I preached the gospel of energy-efficient homes to just about anyone who would listen, but that's all they did. Listen. Or at least pretend to listen. Not Jim. He and I had talked on many occasions about what we thought were the problems with the way houses had traditionally been built. What concerned us most was how much energy those traditionally-built houses wasted. We knew that with the rising cost of fuel it would eventually become extremely important to find a better way to build houses—to construct them so that they used very little energy and almost sustained themselves. At the time of these discussions, green was a color, not a term to describe environmentally-sound construction methods.

When Jim called, I was just finishing up a bachelor's degree in business. But ever since I was a kid, I was fascinated with a construction technique I learned from my father: insulated concrete forms, or ICFs. My dad and uncle sold ICFs and used them in their own business and from them I learned how much sense they made in terms of energy efficiency. I spent a lot of time studying architecture in high school and was probably pretty obnoxious the way I ran my mouth off about how this type of construction technique could change the whole way houses were built. Imagine a teenager on a one-person campaign to change the construction industry. That was me.

Fortunately, I had a lot of wise adults giving me advice. They wanted to make sure that my passion for the environment didn't get me into trouble and better yet, didn't turn people off to what was most important in my message: awareness of a growing problem.

Now that I was about to finish my degree and enter the real world, I wanted to do something special. I realized that all my talk had accomplished nothing. It was time to either put up or shut up, and Jim's call came at the perfect time.

"Why don't you put all that environmental concern to work and build a house for me?"

Of course! Why didn't I think of that? It's one thing to tell everyone why they should build more energy efficient homes. By this time—around 2004—most people *knew* the value of conserving energy. But was it really feasible? Jim's house would be a perfect opportunity to show people of how a house could be built to conserve energy and lessen its load on the planet.

Making fuel companies angry

We jumped in with both feet and in the end, the house was everything that we had hoped it would be. It was beautiful, came in on budget, and most important, took very little fuel to heat it in the cold winter months. So little, in fact, that we made the fuel company angry. In this particular area, the fuel of choice is propane. Propane companies install a huge tank on the property and happily keep it filled with their expensive fuel. Most homes require the company to come out and fill the tank at least once a year—sometimes more often. But the house we built was so efficient that my cousin only had to buy propane every other year!

We learned one of our very first valuable lessons about propane companies through this. Their business model is based on putting homeowners on a buying plan. They knew approximately when a tank would need to be filled and automatically showed up to fill it. This created a reliable revenue stream. Customers like Jim were a problem—so much so that he had a hard time finding a company to sell him propane because he didn't fit their buying plan.

In other words, the propane industry depended on energy-sucking homes for their success. This was an eye opener to me and was a blatant indicator that there was a problem with energy efficiency in the building industry. Jim's house was built to provide a warm, comfortable, attractive home and he got that.

Social Media Callout Box

*(Post the sentence below
to your social media account.)*

*What the industry gained
was a real life example
that a house could be built
on a normal budget with
low energy bills.*

What the industry gained was a real life example that a house could be built for a normal budget that had ridiculously low energy bills. This house started what would be part of an incredible transformation in an industry that badly needed a change.

It's not entirely the construction industry's fault. For years, energy costs were so low that people were content to purchase houses built with minimal insulation and maximum amenities. Why go through the trouble and expense of building energy-efficient homes if the cost of energy was barely noticeable?

What made Jim's house so important is not just the ICFs that were used as the exterior shell, but that the house was built at such an important time in history. We started building this house in 2005. At the beginning of that year, the average price of gasoline was $2.61 per gallon. Then Hurricane Katrina struck, damaging refineries and sending the price of gas soaring. And they just keep climbing, which has caused everyone to consider finding ways to save on fuel costs—not just for their cars, but for their homes as well.

As I write this, gas prices in my home state of Michigan are just under $4.00 a gallon, and experts are talking about $5.00 per gallon in the very near future. Whether you heat with natural gas, propane, or heating oil, you most likely have noticed higher bills with each passing year, and all the experts are predicting they will continue to rise. When you combine the rising cost of fuel and the devastating effects of a poor economy, it's easy to see why word spread quickly that I was building a new kind of house—one that would give people relief from their soaring energy bills. A local designer and I had become friends through our similar views in life and housing design. It was through this designer that I got a lead to build an ICF house that would ignite the explosive growth of my company, Hybrid Homes, LLC.

But not everyone was as supportive of my efforts to build energy efficient homes. For example, I asked one local lumber company to stock a number of "green" products to improve availability. The president of the lumber company called me into his office, sat me down, and closed his door. After a short silence, he said, "Look, I love your enthusiasm for this stuff, but I can't stock this stuff in our store because it could alienate our other builders." After this conversation, I chose to use another lumber company that was as excited about equipping the building industry to change as I was.

Supply companies who were not willing to stock the new, soon-to-be-called "green" products, actually helped unite those of us who wanted to lead a change in the building industry. There were a small number of individuals who hoped a change would come about in the building industry, a change that would lead to the building of energy efficient, occupant-friendly houses. Companies that were willing to stock these environmentally friendly products for businesses like mine soon found themselves gaining new customers and increasing their revenues, while other supply companies were noticing a serious drop in sales due to a sluggish economy.

I was once told by one of those wise people in my life that the way to change an industry is to create a trend that would lead to new demand. Creating a trend didn't sound like such a tough thing to do, so on the morning that I left to start building another house, I said these words out loud: "Well, it's time to go to seal my fate." They proved to be prophetic words because they set in motion a whirlwind in my life that would take years to get under control.

The house we planned to build was selected as a show house in a renewable energy fair. This house was cutting edge, and would be the first LEED platinum level house ever built in the state of Michigan. I had no idea what I was doing, but I had a wealth of book smarts and an unquenchable thirst for adventure and the unknown. Little did I know that I would spend a year and a half living in a town far from my home, learning on the job.

Not everyone is green

One of the things I learned is that not everyone is crazy about saving the environment. As we were almost finished building the home, I received a phone call from our home office, informing me that a letter had just arrived from the township. As I was read the letter over the phone, my jaw hit the ground. The letter said that I was in violation of a township ordinance for putting up a residential wind generator in an area that did not allow such a device. This was a surprise, because I actually did have the blessing of the township to have the wind generator installed. A neighbor to the project had found a loophole and started a long, expensive battle that I had not planned on fighting.

This was an extremely lonely time in my life. I had been pretty vocal about building a project that no one thought was possible, and now I was in newspapers being called a rogue builder who runs rough shod over local ordinances. I thought I had enough fight in my blood to go to battle with my own time and money for this wind generator to remain as part of the house. But within a few months after the renewable energy fair and as the season was turning to fall, I ran out of money and had just one employee who was helping me finish this incredible, industry changing house. Although the company was still drawing a wage for each of us to work on the house, the mounting costs of fighting for the wind generator was taking every penny I had.

Navigating the "bleeding edge of technology" can be a tough road to take, but I set out to start a trend and I was stubborn enough to go as far as I could before I crashed and burned. One day I walked through town and entered the one grocery store in this small village. As I walked in, people in the store turned their backs to me. I thought it odd, not realizing it was in response to a front-page article about the wind generator fiasco in the local newspaper. The next morning, after bringing back beer cans for the deposit money, I went into a restaurant for breakfast, and there was a table of people talking about me. Half of the table were members of the same township board that two nights prior had slammed a gavel down and forbade anyone from talking about the wind generator outside of the township hall. Yet they sat with their friends and discussed the case and how it violated the township ordinance for wind generators.

In late 2007, not many people knew about the problems associated with putting up wind generators in residential areas. A term was coined around this time, NIMBY, which stands for Not In My Back Yard. Projects likes ours started to make the front page of newspapers all over the country, and that exposure helped to get more and more people to research renewable energy in their areas. I knew that battling the township on my own dime would be a powerful experience, but I had no idea that it would help to reshape residential renewable energy as everyone had known it.

There were a few reasons why I was passionate about the wind generator on this project. For starters, the zoning administrator knew well in advance that we were building a home that would have a wind generator. Luckily, since most of our communication was documented in email, I felt emboldened to press the issue to the point that I did.

Another reason why I was so passionate about the wind generator is that it was built in a place where it would actually work. The project is high above Lake Michigan, where the winds blow constantly. Wind generators don't work in very many places, but this project was a perfect test case. I didn't want to see it taken down because I knew it would help convince people that wind was a legitimate source of electricity.

Ultimately, after six months of battling, a deal was struck and the wind generator was allowed at the project site. As part of the deal, it had to be moved 100 feet to the north because the neighbors were afraid that ice might spin off of the blades and damage property or injure people. This entire ordeal had moments that made me laugh—the things that people say. One argument against the turbine was that the neighbors were afraid that their kids were going to get sucked up into the relatively small residential wind turbine and killed!

Gaining momentum

The exposure that we gained from this project was extraordinary! The phone began to ring off the hook, as the economic recession and soaring gas prices fueled new interest in energy saving homes. Before I knew it, I was traveling the state of Michigan meeting with homeowners who were interested in building hybrid houses. Just after we finished the house south of Traverse City, we began two new projects—one in southwest Michigan and the other in western Michigan, close to Lake Michigan. The house in southwest Michigan was very similar to the Traverse City project, while the house in western Michigan would be built out of a different material, Structural Insulated Panels, or SIPs, as they are known as in the building industry.

It was a very interesting time to be a builder in the state of Michigan. Our company was growing by leaps and bounds, renewable energy companies were popping up, and the state government was spending most of its time and money working to improve its renewable energy position. Consumers became extremely interested in what we were doing. The federal government offered tax credits for many of the innovative solutions our company (and few others) were delivering. The world seemed to be moving at an incredible pace toward the destination I had long evangelized, and we were right in the middle of it all!

Our experience building ICF homes made the southwest Michigan project fairly easy, and only required a couple employees. To tackle the home near Lake Michigan, I hired a framing company to install the SIPs.

As we worked on these projects, more and more people would call, looking for us to build or consult with them on their houses. I would dedicate part of each day to answering and returning phone calls. This activity added many hours to my day, and I still needed to visit the active jobsites each day to ensure any questions were being addressed and that the houses were being put together properly.

Efficiency became the key focus during the building process. We finished building an entire hybrid home with basically two people, a homeowner, and a handful of sub-contractors. I was determined to reach our overall goal of building an energy efficient home for the price of a conventional home. As a team, we learned that the building materials selected to build a

> **Social Media Callout Box**
> *(Post the sentence below to your social media account.)*
>
> ***We finished building an entire hybrid home with two people, a homeowner, and a handful of sub-contractors.***

home should be based on reducing labor costs while not compromising the integrity of the overall project. I pushed our crews to create new efficiencies, and as a team, we learned ways to save incredible amounts of time on a project without sacrificing quality, energy efficiency, or material grade.

That's what this book is all about—to share what I have learned so that if you plan on having a new home built, you can put these energy-saving methods to work.

Eventually, our team had built, back-to-back national award winning LEED for Homes platinum level houses. Our company made the cover of many national publications and I was recognized as a leader in green and sustainable building. What was once considered too edgy was becoming a part of everyday talk in the building industry. While the business was moving forward at an accelerated pace, my goal was still fresh on my mind: "To build a super energy efficient home at the price of a normal home."

While we were finishing the two houses mentioned above, I signed contracts to build four very unique homes. The fact that we had successfully built an SIP house that was awarded a LEED for Homes platinum home led to more houses made with SIPs. From this increased workload, I was able to start combining technologies to see how they worked with each other. Soon we were building with ICF basements and SIP above ground walls. On a challenge, we built an advanced framed house with an ICF basement that achieved incredible results in energy efficiency, so much so, that it completely changed the way I thought about building.

And I want to share it all with you. Whether you are a builder, a person looking to have a new home built, or an enthusiast about saving the environment, you will find a wealth of information here that will convince you it's possible to enjoy a nice, comfortable home that is not only good for the planet, but easy on your budget.

2 WHY WE DO WHAT WE DO

Throughout my life, I often wondered why I acted the way I did, or why someone would buy one product over another. The reasons weren't apparent; I decided that I needed to go to college to have others teach me the things that I could not figure out myself. I read somewhere that you can't manage others or a business until you can manage yourself. Reading that one line in a book changed my life and was the reason why I finally signed up at the local community college where I lived. My ideas for the marketing of my building business were shaped during and after I went to school for a business and marketing degree.

My education at the local community college was incredible. I can say that I learned more about running a business and realizing an idea from the instructors who taught me there than when I went on to a university. These community college instructors had their own companies, or ran companies for others, and gave me more than just their take on the words in a book. They were willing to give me advice and share their perspective on life in business if I asked them. I stayed after class every day to talk to the instructors to figure out why I had such a strong draw to start my own company. All I ever wanted to hear was the bad stuff about business, but what I learned is that business success is relative to the work you put into it. You will see that in the story that unfolds in this book.

Hybrid Homes started as a project that I did in one of my marketing classes. I launched Hybrid Homes after I learned how successful the company could be, based on the research that I had done for my project. I was working as a mobile disc jockey (DJ) while I went to school to pay for the classes. Aside from all the wedding receptions that people are still talking about to this day, I had the privilege of working for a guy who was one of the top marketers in the country. Whether he knew it or not, I thought of him as my marketing mentor, and would constantly bounce my marketing ideas off of him.

His name is Greg Stielstra and he shared chapters of a book he was writing with me during the beginning stages of my business. His book, *PyroMarketing,* became one of the resources that I used for the marketing of Hybrid Homes. *PyroMarketing* gave me valuable insight into effective strategic marketing. Greg's book and my schooling developed an even greater longing to learn why people made the decisions that they made in their lives.

As I progressed through school, read *PyroMarketing*, and researched peoples' behavioral patterns, one thing kept coming up: motivation. Motivation is the key to all of the decisions that people make, big and small. What I learned was that everyone is different in their logic and therefore has different

> ### Social Media Callout Box
> *(Post the sentence below to your social media account.)*
>
> ***Motivation is the key to all of the decisions that people make, big and small.***

motivations for making the decisions that they do. Marketers have done a great job of generalizing people and their motivations into groups that they then market products too. This generalizing doesn't always work though, especially when the marketers are trying to market a home. I learned that mass marketing works well for products like soft drinks and potato chips, but would not work very well for custom energy efficient homes.

As you drive around your town, there are most likely development companies pitching inexpensive houses. These residences are usually lacking in features and are homes the buyers settle for. Neighborhoods full of inexpensive, no frills homes can be found in nearly every state in the U.S., and despite the economic downturn, these inexpensive homes continue to sell.

How could it be that in a time with historic home foreclosures and a surplus of inexpensive foreclosed houses on the market, a person would still choose to buy a new home? Doesn't it seem unusual that a buyer would select a new house for $250,000 and not a foreclosed house for $30,000? The key is that big builders know what potential buyers need to see and feel when they tour a home.

Motivation is what drives people's decisions. Many buyers who purchase inexpensive homes in the neighborhoods mentioned above do so for a few reasons. These reasons can be: the house meets or falls below their budget; the house is in a school district they like; and/or the buyer was specifically looking to buy or build a brand new house. The people who buy these kinds of homes can be generalized into a group of people who share similar tastes and motivations. What I have found is that this group of buyers will react to a specific marketing plan, but this marketing plan does not work on different buyer groups.

I believe that when an economy slips into a recession, it is because of buyer motivation. Persistent news coverage of a failing economy causes the need for financial security and other safety needs to dominate a person's thoughts. People will typically start spending less money on things they don't *need*, and divert that money to savings to help create a feeling of financial security. This financial security will help to confirm that the needs for food, water, paying the rent, and any other physiological needs are met.

As I was developing this theory on the economy, there was one question that kept bouncing around inside my head: Why, if a person is slipping into a defensive position during a downturn in the economy, would they ever consider building a new home? The answer I discovered was once again very simple: motivation. That question lead to another question that I pondered: Why, if there are millions of homes sitting vacant in the country due to foreclosure, would someone ever consider building a new home that costs more money than if they bought a foreclosed home? The answer is again was quite simple: motivation.

Turning a passion into a business

To understand this point better, consider the following real life example of how a company recognized a way to understand buyer motivation and thus saw great growth as a result: Fresh out of a community college with associate's degrees in marketing and management (and with a fair number of higher-level classes under his belt), a thirty-something business owner was looking for a way to connect with people who saw things the way he saw them. This business owner wanted to build homes that were not only energy efficient, but also environmentally friendly. He wanted this so bad, because he was raised to believe that the earth was a special place, a place that we should all take care of. This builder was motivated to do what he was doing for specific reasons. He was searching for others with the same motivation, and felt that once he found that buyer group, his business would grow and so would the ultimate plan: for people to reduce their impact on the planet.

Okay, this story is about me. As I was searching out likeminded people, I would talk to everyone about my ideas and the need for humans to reduce their load on this planet. While talking to a group of attendees at a home show, I was approached by a designer and his wife, and we immediately became friends. Together, this designer and I discussed many ideas about building and designing green. The designer never met a builder with unfailing confidence in his ability to achieve his dreams, and I had never met a designer or architect who would give me the time of day.

Somewhere along the way, the designer was contacted by a homeowner who wanted to build a cutting edge ICF home somewhere south of Traverse City, Michigan. Since I had built a few ICF projects at this point, I was very interested in taking on this challenge, so the designer gave the potential client my name. I immediately began to ponder the homeowner's motivations. Somewhere along the way, I decided that others must have similar motivations, and I started to look for an event or place where these likeminded people would be.

Serendipitously, my designer friend learned that the ICF home was to be built in the same town as the only renewable energy fair. This renewable energy fair showcased renewable energy and alternative forms of producing goods and energy. I had never heard of this energy fair, but I imagined it could be a key element of our marketing plan, so some reconnaissance was in order.

Without even talking to the potential clients of this potential project, I made plans to visit the energy fair to locate people who shared my passions and motivations.

As a perceptive marketer on a mission, the energy fair would reveal motivations from the moment I entered town . When I pulled into the parking lot at the fairgrounds, I immediately noticed there were no builders in attendance. Builders normally emblazon their vehicles with logos and signage to get free advertising in the parking lot. As I parked my truck (which had no name on it) and walked towards the entry gate, I could not even imagine the impact my visit would have, not only on the rest of my life, but on the building industry in general. I had no idea as I entered the fairgrounds that sunny, hot Saturday in June, that I had stumbled upon a gold mine. I remember that the entry price didn't seem bad, and that my first thought was, "Hmm, there aren't many people here." The first thing I encountered after I walked past the tents at the entrance was what seemed like the tarmac at an airport, a long, hot, lonely looking black top area that had different types of hybrid vehicles parked along it. Looking past the tarmac, I noticed lots of solar panels and tents full of people at the back side of the fairgrounds. I adopted a hurried pace and became anxious as I walked throughout the fairgrounds, listening to the conversations. I heard people talk about protecting the earth, renewable energy, and the main thing I was searching for: people talking about building sustainably. These weren't builders but people who wanted to build energy efficient homes, but who could not find a builder who understood their needs. I was so excited, I could hardly even focus on all of the booths and conversations that people were having, so I stepped away from the exhibition area and picked up my phone. My hands were shaking as I scrolled through the list of names on my phone, looking for my designer friend's number. I called him and said very quickly and nearly out of breath, "I need that job by the energy fair, I'll do whatever I have to do to get it." In his voice he replied, "Ok, I will give him a call."

Before I left the energy fair, I searched out the organizer and introduced myself. I told her my plans, and that I wanted the ICF home to be the headlining attraction at the following year's energy fair. The organizer looked at me like I was crazy and said, "Good luck with that." I just smiled at her; I was no stranger to being called crazy and I could see it all happening in my head. Since no one had ever marketed a green/sustainable house through an energy fair before, the organizer didn't have a clue as to what kind of potential it could bring to her event. As she handed me her card and hurried off to get away from me, I thought, "That went great, now all I need to do is get that job." Leaving town that day, I had no idea what was brewing, and could never have possibly imagined that I would be writing this book, in part, because of my visit to the energy fair.

Shortly after the fair, the mild mannered designer set up an introductory meeting with the ICF-home clients. After that meeting, the designer and I developed a plan to market the client's house in a way that no one in the country had ever done. I was so confident that I would get the job, that I paid someone to redesign my company logo to include a wind generator. Later, several companies added this same look to their logos, but I was happy to be the first one in the state to do it. I championed the logo redesign because the house was going to have a wind generator, and we were fully planning on showing this house in the energy fair the following year.

Now, I had developed a motivation that fueled my desire to take on a project like none before. Not only did I want to build this project, but I was willing to have people who had similar motivations visit the house and critique it. In this manner, our team could learn from those who shared similar passions. It was basically another way to learn what was motivating this buyer group so that we could figure out the best way to service them.

What motivates you?

Although there is a long and lengthy story of how the event transpired and how this original idea to use the energy fair to market a product to a buyer group unfolded, the one key takeaway remains:

motivation. Everyone is motivated differently, but some do share common motivations. The best team will be one that is formed with people who share these similar motivations. Builders, homeowners, suppliers, sub-contractors, and even neighbors can make or break a project. It can be difficult to find those who share similar motivations, but it is more than worth the effort.

The company that I own went on to become nationally recognized for its sustainable building efforts and environmental work. Our seminal project in Traverse City launched at the worst time in a terrible recession, while other builders were closing their doors, but my company grew at an incredible rate. We recognized how to find people who shared similar motivations, and we knew how to service them. If you can think like a buyer

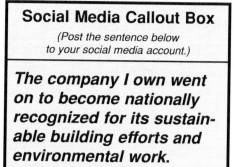

Social Media Callout Box

(Post the sentence below to your social media account.)

The company I own went on to become nationally recognized for its sustainable building efforts and environmental work.

and uncover motivations, the work is there, even in a recession.

Green building programs such as the United States Green Building Council's LEED for Homes program are a great way for homeowners or builders to realize the types of houses they want to build. The LEED for Homes program has a long checklist that ensures a homeowner's home is being built to a certain standard. For a builder, the LEED for Homes program helps guide them through the building of the home, and requires a third-party inspection to confirm the home meets the criteria of the checklist. A green building program such as LEED for Homes outlines accountability that certifies the three stakeholders in the building of the home—the homeowners, the builder, and the environment—are all on the same page. In this manner, the homeowner gets what they paid for, the

WHY WE DO WHAT WE DO

builder has proof that they built the home according to contract, and the house has far less impact on the planet than a conventional home.

Everyone's motivation for doing the things that they do is unique. This book will help you decide if one or more of the concepts, products, or processes deescribed will work for you or someone you know. I have written several chapters on specific building materials and the experience my crews and myself have had with these materials. Even if you are not looking to build or remodel in the near future, the story of how we came to use these products and the pain and suffering and glory that precipitated as a result of using those products is definitely entertaining in the very least. That should be motivation enough to continue reading from here.

3   SUSTAINABLE BUILDING MATERIALS

What makes a product green? Great question! Until recently, lumber companies and other suppliers just stocked conventional products because there was no demand for anything else. When we started putting together the marketing plan for the house near the energy fair, one of the first things we did was sit down with our suppliers and see if we could get the products that we wanted. Most of these suppliers had no idea what we were talking about, or if their suppliers could ever get what we were asking for. I remember literally begging a supplier to get the products that we needed on that energy fair show house. The main reason that suppliers would not stock these green products is because they did not want to alienate their other customers. I understood that, but I also understood that this is what was stalling out the change that I felt was necessary for the building industry.

Green products are those that have less of an impact on the environment or are less detrimental to human health than conventional products. Often they are formed from recycled components or are manufactured in a way that conserves energy.

Presently, you can't walk through a big-box store or lumber company and see very little green building materials. But that is rapidly changing. Every

> **Social Media Callout Box**
> *(Post the sentence below to your social media account.)*
>
> ***Just because a product is labeled green doesn't always mean it's environmentally friendly.***

time you go to the gas station to fuel up your vehicle, you are reminded of how much it costs to use things. This awareness is higher than ever before, and that is why the demand for green products is at an all-time high. But just because a product is labeled green doesn't always mean it's environmentally friendly, which has led to a new term in the industry known as "green washing"—the practice of making an unsubstantiated claim about a product's environmental benefit.

Shades of green

It's great to see so many green products in stores all over the country, but with all of these products you still need to do your homework to make sure you are getting a product that is truly environmentally friendly. There are many factors to consider. First, you must look at what the product is made out of. The material should be a renewable resource or manufactured in a facility that is environmentally friendly. Next, you should look at the maintenance profile of the product. If a person is looking to build a sustainable house, then the products they use on and in the house should require very little maintenance and should last a very long time. There were several companies that raced to get their products to market but did not give much thought to maintenance and lifecycle. Be certain to study the maintenance on the green products that you are considering buying.

Bamboo was one of the first mainstream "green" products to come on the market. Everybody jumped on the bamboo bandwagon until the truth about the harvesting and manufacturing of bamboo products hit the news. Bamboo grows very quickly and can be harvested after only five years of growth. The majority of the bamboo currently used in products is grown, harvested, and manufactured in

China, which has no environmental protection agency. Adhesives used on most bamboo products contain urea-formaldehyde, which emits formaldehyde into the air. Formaldehyde has been known to cause a number of illnesses in humans, the worst being different forms of cancer. There *is* safe bamboo on the market; all it takes is a little research to locate which bamboo brands use non-formalde-hyde adhesives.

Mainstream media promoted the idea that bamboo flooring was green, but once I learned that China had no environmental protection agency and that other problems have occurred as the result of the growth and harvesting of bamboo, I became suspect of products made of bamboo. I learned that bamboo has become a profitable crop for farmers to grow; as a result, many acres of wooded forests have been clear cut to grow bamboo. Another major problem I discovered is the pollution that is released into the rivers as the result of manufacturing products out of bamboo. Rivers in China are used for many things, including bathing and drinking, and reports have shown that the residents of villages along these contaminated rivers have shown an increase in illnesses.

Hidden dangers

There are several green building programs available today that do a great job of listing methods and products that are environmentally friendly. Those green building programs also offer ways of improving each stage of the building process. For instance, before a house is built, a lot must be cleared to make room for the house. Our team always thought that a good rule of thumb is to plant two trees for every one tree that you must remove to make room for a house.

This makes trees and shrubs a sustainable/green product, as long as the homeowner selects the proper trees and shrubs for their climate and area.

In many areas of the country, there is a hidden gas that is the second leading cause of lung cancer in the United States: radon. Radon is a gas that seeps into homes through the basement or crawl-space. Radon forms from the natural breakdown of uranium and can also be found in ground water. Due to the threat of radon in homes, people looking to build a sustainable/green house must research the area where they intend to build to determine radon risk. To learn where the radon risk areas are in the United States, go to www.epa.gov/radon/zonemap.html.

If a person is building a house in a moderate- to high-risk area for radon, they must take measures to vent the home of potential radon gas seepage. One of the best ways that I have found to do this is to run perforated drain tile around all of the footings on the inside of the house, in addition to the drain tile run on the outside of the house footings. Connect the entire footing drain tile on the inside of the house footings together and run it to a three-inch diameter PVC pipe. Run the PVC pipe up through the house, through the attic space and vent it out of the roof as one would a plumbing vent. Additionally, many green building rating programs recommend the installation of an inline fan on the PVC pipe to draw the radon up and out of the house.

I once read somewhere that basement walls can account for an average of twenty percent of the energy costs of a home. Un-insulated poured concrete walls and masonry block walls offer no insulation to the cold temperature of winter months, and can heat up during the warm summer months. To see how many homes have very little to no insulation in their basements, all you have to do is drive by a sub-division and look for houses with walk out base-ments that have exposed foundation walls. There is a very good chance that the exposed walls you see are un-insulated and are cool or cold to the touch in the wintertime.

Many states have adopted energy codes that now require basement walls to be insulated to a certain performance level. Besides the traditional concrete block and poured concrete foundation, there are other products and processes available for insulated foundation and basement walls. These products include insulated poured wall systems, insulated concrete block systems, and a system that I referred to earlier and will be discussed later in this book in great detail, insulated concrete forms (ICFs). There aren't many building products on the market that can save a person twenty percent of their heating and/or cooling costs. I believe that is what makes buying the right product for a foundation one of the most important purchases on a project. Controlling consumption is the key to a sustainable home, and with the right foundation, the homeowner automatically consumes less energy and saves money. With the basement walls accounting for up to twenty percent of a home's heating and cooling costs, the remaining costs to

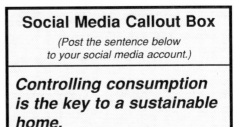

heat and cool a home are split up between the exterior walls and roof systems.

Seal the envelope

The most important part of a house when it comes to energy savings is its exterior walls and roof system, otherwise known as the house's *envelope*. There are several options when it comes to the exterior walls of a home. A traditional "stick-built" (wood-framed) home has minimal insulation and maximum air flow through the walls, resulting in very high heating and cooling costs. On a 2x4 wall with normal insulation, the r-value is R-13. R-value is a measure of how a material impedes heat flow with a higher number indicating a greater resistance to heat flow. A stick built wall with R-13 batt insulation is a poorly insulated wall compared to other systems or forms of insulation on the market. While r-value is only one of many different readings on a house (and that r-value can be misleading), it is a widely known term, and will serve this book well for purposes of example

To understand the performance of building materials, one must consider the entire *system* that is in place. A system model takes into consideration every component. In other words, if you build a house out of a list of materials, those materials should complement the other materials that are used on the house. For a house that has an exterior wall framed with 2x4s and insulated with fiberglass batt insulation, I would expect that system to perform in the following way:

Every material used works with and against the other material used in the system. The average stick-built exterior wall has the following materials as a part of it: 1/2" drywall (r-value of .45), 2x4

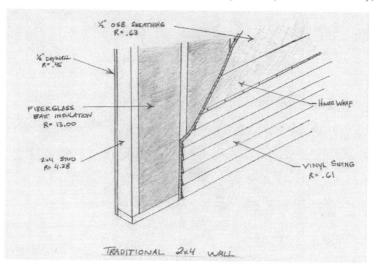

TRADITIONAL 2x4 WALL

studs (r-value of 4.38), fiberglass batt insulation (r-value of 13.00), 1/2"plywood or OSB sheathing (r-value of .63), and vinyl siding (r-value of .61).

When all of these materials are combined, a traditional 2x4 stick built wall carries an r-value of approximately R-14.69 (between the 2x4 walls studs). Sounds impressive, but here's the problem: every sixteen inches or so, something important happens—there is no insulation. The insulation is stapled to the wall stud, which means that you lose R-13 at every stud. The other building materials listed do carry an r-value (as indicated above), but it only equates to about R-6.07. This means that a good portion of a traditional 2x4 stick-built exterior wall only carries an r-value of 6.07, and creates a system where the insulation is not continuous. (Note: House wraps are required by most codes but can affect the insulating properties of an exterior wall in different ways, so it is not discussed in this book or figured into the r-value of the example wall.) This allows thermal pass-through of the wall studs and the materials attached to them and explains why a person can walk up to an exterior wall in their home and feel that it is cold to the touch during the cold months of the year.

Building is part of a system wherein each component of a house interacts positively or negatively with the others. In the example above, the traditional 2x4 stick-built house leads to insulation problems. Such problems can go undetected for years until the structure of the home becomes compromised, or the people in the home start noticing health problems. Improperly sealed homes can cause frost inside wall cavities where the sheathing meets the sill plate. There are many examples where nails used to secure wall studs rusted apart from wintertime frost buildup. Great attention must be paid to ensure that air penetration of an exterior wall is minimal.

Even if we do our best to seal the house properly—referred to as making it tight—we still need to watch for even the tiniest of air leaks. One very cold Michigan morning, I visited one of our advanced framed houses with my dad and during our walk through, we made a shocking discovery in the basement.

Although the basement was made of ICFs, there was a small portion of the walkout wall that had been stick framed. Every one of the anchor bolts that were securing that wall portion to the foundation were completly covered in a thick layer of frost. Upon further investigation, I noticed that freezing cold air was racing through a small gap under the sill plate wherever there was an anchor bolt securing the wall to the foundation. The house was so tight, that even these small leaks became a huge problem. Can you imagine how many stick-framed houses in the world have this undetected problem? This could be the reason why most houses have some form of rotting in the walkout area.

I will be explaining several options that will improve the tightness of the exterior envelope of a home, including the four most widely used forms of exterior envelope construction: Insulated Concrete Forms (ICFs), Structural Insulated Panels (SIPs), Advanced Framing, and Earth Shelter. But first a word about insulation.

That fluffy pink stuff

There was a time in the not-so-distant past when builders simply put pink fiberglass insulation in an attic and the walls of a house and called it good. It was okay, but not very energy efficient. But the cost of energy to heat and cool houses in the U.S. was traditionally low, and consequently not much attention was paid to insulation. Most builders bathe in tradition—stepping out of the box to focus more attention on how to properly insulate a house wasn't on their to-do list.

I learned the hard way that if you cut corners on insulation and its proper installation, it can come back to haunt you. For example, I recall a particular house that was built as tight as a house of its design could be built . . . or so I thought. The house was built entirely of ICFs and had trusses and framed rafters for the roof system. We used open cell spray foam in the attic area, and knew from past experience that this spray foam insulation was a great compliment to a house built out of ICFs. Because the roof system combined trusses with rafters, the roof was complex in design and included a lot of lumber. At the time, we had great success in spraying the foam to the top side of the ceiling drywall. The design of the roof on this house prevented us from being able to spray foam to the top of the drywall in some areas of the house. On other homes we built, we had sprayed foam to the bottom side of the roof deck and had good results, so we tried that in areas of this particular house.

One frosty Fall morning, I received a call from the homeowner, who asked me to come out and look at his frosty morning roof to see where the heat was leaking. When my early morning schedule cleared enough to permit a visit I used a thermal imaging camera on the attic area to discover where warm air from inside the house was leaking through the roof. There were several spots where heat was transferring from inside the attic space, through a piece of framing lumber, and right to the outside.

The problem? Although I used the best possible method of insulating this house, I wasn't present to oversee the application. I learned sometimes the lower-paid employees who performed the installation work rushed to finish the job, often missing critical areas. From that point on I always made sure to inspect the areas that they worked on while the project owners were onsite so that any problems could be corrected immediately and not on a return visit. I did this constantly with insulation, and made sure that while the hoses were out and while all the plastic was up to protect the other work from the spray foam, workers took care of any problems as they arose—it was more efficient that way for everyone. I highly recommend this practice: always inspect work while the crews are there and set up. Repairs or adjustments can be handled quickly and painlessly to all involved.

If a home is to be stick built, spray foam insulation can be a great compliment to that system. To avoid hazardous off gasses, agricultural-based spray foams should be used instead of the other petroleum-based spray foams. These agricultural spray foams are temperamental and require an experienced installer to ensure the installation is done properly. Specific temperature and atmospheric conditions are required to enable proper expansion and setting of the foam.

Soy-based spray foams are a popular option, but they are not without their problems. Everyone in the green movement used soy-based foams when they first came out. What everyone learned later was that soybean crops vary, and so did the quality of the resultant soy foams. Poor soybean crop quality resulted in spray foams that rapidly broke down, leaving home owners with attics and walls full of useless soy dust.

There are all sorts of insulation products available on the market, some quite innovative. In fact, there is a company that sponsors the collection of worn out blue jeans, which are then re-purposed into insulation. Coolness factor aside, if the cost of recycled blue jean insulation weren't so high, we certainly would have used it in our homes. Fiberglass batt insulation is still on the market and popular—we still use it for sound proofing or for other interior insulation projects. No matter what form of insulation you choose to use, just remember that it is part of the system that you are building. Never skimp

> **Social Media Callout Box**
> *(Post the sentence below to your social media account.)*
>
> ***Never skimp on insulation because it is one of the most important parts of the building system.***

on insulation because it is one of the most important parts of the building system. There are better areas of the home to target for cost savings, and if you have any control over the project, select the best available insulation products.

Windows: energy escape hatch?

Prevalent thermal images available on the internet reveal that windows are the biggest breach of the entire envelope system. Therefore, windows are not the place where you should try to save money. A poor quality window can make or break an energy efficient home. To learn more about how windows work, why they are so important, and what the numbers mean on the window labels, I tracked down architect Daniel Grubish of the Andersen Window Corporation in Bayport, Minnesota. Here's what he had to say:

> Windows play a very important part in the exterior envelope of a home because they provide: protection against the elements, natural ventilation, natural lighting and connection to the outdoors. When in the selection process, don't assume the cheapest product will serve you well and don't fall for the misnomer that "one size fits all. Beyond price, be sure to consider: architectural style, operational type, material types, glazing types, hardware and trim options. Investigate the manufacturer's innovation track record and durability of

windows and doors they manufacture. Also study the manu-facturer's warranty and service performance over the years, as opposed to recent claims. Verify the manufacturer's standing in the industry and the manufacturer's history of environmental stewardship. The thing to remember is that given your budget, the home you are building should be designed and built to remain functional and comfortable for as long as possible. Selecting improper windows may reduce the length of time the home can live up to the high standards you both want and deserve.

There are key industry performance values you should consider when selecting windows: thermal performance, structural resistance to wind forces, and resistance to water and air infiltration. The National Fenestration Rating Council (NFRC) and the Window and Door Manufacturers Association (WDMA) developed industry testing standards for these performance values as an "apples-to-apples" way for you to compare the multitude of manufacturers and their various windows. A good manufacturer will provide their tested values as part of their products' reference materials for easier access. The builder need only compare the values during window selection to help determine which window will work best for the home's intended design and long-term performance. The manufacturer's performance values will be noted on the NFRC label, which is required to be placed on the glass of each window. The NFRC label proves to the home inspector the window has been independently tested and certified to industry standards and/or complies with spe-cific building code requirements.

What are these values and what do they mean in layman's terms?

- **U-Factor** is the resistance of heat in a room escaping through the window to the exterior. The lower the value the more resistance and therefore the more it helps reduce heating requirements.

- **Solar Heat Gain Coefficient** is the resistance of heat from the sun transferred through the window into the room. The lower the value the more resistance and therefore the more it helps reduce air conditioning requirements.

- **Visible Transmittance** is how much visible light transfers through the glazing system. The higher the value the more visible light is transmitted.

- **Performance Grade (PG)** is the window's maximum resistance to wind forces measured in pounds per square feet (PSF) and directly tied to water and air infiltration. The higher the value the more resistance to wind-blown elements.

  It needs to be noted that for all these values, the level of tested performance is affected by: window type, frame materials, cladding materials and glazing types. The size of the window can also affect one or more of the values during testing so a builder should compare as many aspects of a window as they can when doing a side-by-side comparison between manufacturers.

The numbers on the windows do mean something, as Dan said. As I mentioned above, windows are a very important part of the system when it comes to building an energy efficient house. If you insist on going with an inexpensive window in your house, keep the information that Dan has written above in mind and at least try to get as close as you can afford to a window that will perform well in your house.

Up on the roof

One of my favorite things to do is look at the different roof styles on homes I drive past. I do this because I try to imagine how well those roof systems are insulated. I look on frosty mornings to see how complex roof systems are performing and if they are leaking any heat from the home. I also look to compare the roof designs of the homes we have built to similar styles that others have built to see how our projects stand up to the competition.

One of the most important areas of a home to consider during the design stage of a home is the roof system. Roofs that have several valleys and different lines translate into an incredible amount of framing in that roof system. Houses that have these types of complicated roof lines often have icicles in the winter, because heat from the conditioned areas of a home can heat these framing members up. Excess framing material makes it very hard to insulate these areas, and allows the framing members to heat the snow on the roof above the framing. All it takes is for the framing member to be one degree above freezing to start melting snow or ice, as I have learned the hard way.

Social Media Callout Box

(Post the sentence below to your social media account.)

All it takes is for the framing member to be one degree above freezing to start melting snow or ice.

If a roof system is built properly and insulated properly, then the difference between the interior of the attic area and the exterior should only be a few degrees. This holds true for every day of the year. If a roof system is extremely hot in the summertime, then chances are, the roof has a ventilation problem. There are different codes in each state to consider when figuring the ventilation of a roof system. It is very important for a roof system to be properly ventilated, because proper ventilation can extend the life of shingles and other building materials. Roof systems with poor ventilation often times lead to ice backup, leaking roofs, and increased energy costs.

Based on my experience and the houses that we have built, one of my favorite roof styles is the hip roof. A hip roof with two- to three-foot overhangs can provide incredible ventilation if the builder knows what they are doing. The trick here is to use vented soffit everywhere around the house and install ridge vents at all the ridges. With the hip roof system, the attic insulation should be installed directly on top of the ceiling drywall. Of all of the options for insulating an attic space, agricultural-based spray foam is what we have found to be an optimal green choice for any type of roof system, including the hip roof system. By ventilating and insulating this way, we expect the attic temperature to be within a few degrees of the outside temperature, any time—and it is.

A roof system that has more than an average amount of framing due to a difficult roof line may require the builder to insulate with spray foam directly to the bottom side of the roof sheathing, with no air space between the insulation and sheathing. In the past, traditional builders may have seen this practice as taboo (like I did), although it is proven to work very well in many homes. Once I saw how effective insulating this way could be with complicated roof systems, I was sold! The idea is that when you spray to the bottom of the roof deck, all ventilation to the roof system is closed. The attic space will warm up like the rest of the house, and no heat will escape through the roof. Insulating this way may require that a supply and return line for the furnace in the home be installed into the sealed attic space. We have had great success insulating living space that is built into the roof system of the home. This is the only way that I have found to keep these attic rooms warm during the cold months and cool during the warm months.

Cool roofs

After researching products to incorporate into the energy fair show house, we decided on a shingle that was considered a "cool roof." (To learn more about what a cool roof is, visit **www.cool-roofs.org**.) Asphalt shingle manufacturers, aware of a growing market opportunity, began developing shingles that kept attic spaces cool. While shingles are usually not the main reason for a hot attic space, this new generation of shingles definitely couldn't hurt. Most new reflective shingles have top-facing components that reflect the sun's heat away from the shingle, instead of storing the heat like all other shingles.

These new "cool" shingles came about as a result of the United States Environmental Protection Agency's (EPA) "Cool Roofs" Program. In some areas of the country, cool roofs can save a homeowner fifty cents per square foot of roof space on their energy bills. This is one of the efforts the EPA is advancing to lower energy usage in residential homes. I believe, as I have said many times, that a house should be built as a system, where everything used on that house works with the other components of the house. With that said, shingles should not be the only component that makes a roof cool. These cool roof shingles should be combined with a well-ventilated roof system and attic to achieve maximum performance.

Metal roofs seem to be the roof of choice for some designers and architects, because metal keeps the roof system cool during the hot summer months and sheds snow very well in the winter months. Big problems with metal roofs include cost, and finding qualified installers who will warranty their work. While it varies around the country, it is a concern that is keeping people from using metal roofs on their homes. I remember going around in circles with one of our designers because he wanted to use a metal roof on every house that we worked on together. I tried to explain to him about the cost, and that it was tough to find a company that would install the metal roof properly. As a result, we have houses with metal roofs and houses with shingles, and both perform very well because the roof coverings are complimenting the other components of the system of those houses.

The popularity of specific roof coverings is regional in nature. A tile roof or a cedar shake roof can both be very good roof coverings, if installed properly and in the right areas of country. The cedar shake roof, however, requires an extreme attention to detail to prevent leaking, so if you are considering a cedar shake roof on your house, you must find a company that has proven cedar shake installation experience. Consideration should always be given to how much maintenance the roof covering will require over the life of the home. This is a major reason why metal roofing is the preferred roof covering of leading green designers and architects from around the country.

Maintenance-free siding

Siding is usually selected based on the style of the home and the budget. Vinyl siding is used more widely than any other form of siding. In the advanced framing chapter of this book, you will learn how vinyl siding can be installed atop a thermal breaking sheet of foam to complement the system of the advanced framed house. Vinyl siding can also be ordered with foam pre-attached, and this can help reduce thermal pass-through in exterior walls.

In my opinion, all sustainable homes should utilize exterior products that require very little maintenance. A great alternative to cedar siding is cement board siding. Cement board siding can be installed over any form of exterior envelope construction and does not require the maintenance that wood siding requires.

Cement board patterns depend on the company that manufactures the product. One manufacturer produces a cement board product with a frequently repeating pattern, which requires the installer to pay close attention so that a wall does not have a number of the same boards next to each other. All companies have great products, and the ultimate choice of which brand will be used on a house depends on the house's design and the builder's preference. In my experience, there is a noticeable difference between houses that use siding with a close repeating pattern, and those that don't. I always chose the cement board siding with the better, non-repeating pattern.

What about the yard?

If there is one thing that I believe to the core, is that living a sustainable life has everything to do with controlling consumption. Landscaping around the home is no different. You should consider how much water each plant requires to grow when you are buying plants for your landscaping. To reduce the amount of water that a landscaping plan requires, you should look to plant indigenous flora. Indigenous species will thrive because they are used to the climate around your home. Drought-tolerant plants should also be used, and the amount of turf around the house should be limited. The goal is to use little to no water on the landscaping. If you are interested in learning what plants are indigenous to your area, you can hire a

---

Social Media Callout Box

(Post the sentence below to your social media account.)

The goal is to use little to no water on the landscaping

---

landscaper to help you, or you can drive around an area like I do and photograph the local landscape.

Another major consideration in developing a sustainable lifestyle is safe pest control. To keep insects and other pests from getting close to your house without using poison, plants should never be planted closer than twenty-four inches from the base of a house. Plants can be a perfect staging area for pests before they enter a home. Most invasive insects are nomadic, and will move to ideal environments often in order to find the optimal place for their lifestyles. This can mean two things: one, mulch and other products that help keep the ground moist can house several invasive pests (that is why it is not a good idea to use mulch around houses with a lot of ground cover and shrubs); two, if we know that pests are attracted to these types of situations, then we can control pests, in part, by removing their ideal environments.

As each day goes by, more and more natural pest controls become available. Each dangerous product that is applied on or around there home can ultimately affect the homeowners. Using natural pest control measures is another way to keep the homeowners safe and will help in living a sustainable life. I can't over-emphasize this point: natural pest control is part of the overall system of building a sustainable lifestyle.

Okay, that pretty much takes care of the overall structure of the house and yard. As you have learned, decisions about how to build your home can have a huge impact on the environment. But what about inside the house? Does green go inside as well as outside your home?

4 GOING GREEN INDOORS

I believe that the interior of the house is where most of the emphasis should be put for green products. After all, it is where the homeowners will likely spend the majority of their time. Maintaining a healthy environment inside the home is absolutely vital to a healthy sustainable lifestyle, and is as important as the healthy nourishment that you should be putting into your body.

There are infinite choices now for green products that go inside a house. I am going to cover just a few of the most important interior products and/or materials. Take what you learn here and apply it to products or areas of the home that are not discussed in this section of the book.

There are several products that can 'off-gas' in the home, and this off-gassing has caused many illnesses, including chronic coughing and even certain forms of cancer. According to www.natureneutral.com, *"Off-gassing is the evaporation of volatile chemicals in non-metallic materials at normal atmospheric pressure. This means that building materials release chemicals into the air through evaporation. This evaporation can continue for years after the products are initially installed which means you continue to breathe these chemicals as you work, sleep, and relax in your home or office."* This explanation is scary enough to me to insist, without exception, that we only install healthy products and materials into the houses that we build.

Proper ventilation in a home will be discussed in the later chapters of this book. Until then, keep in mind how potentially unhealthy off-gassing products can be in a house that is built incredibly tight and draft free. This can be dangerous to those who live in the home, and explains why there is such a huge push to sell products that don't off-gas. When selecting products for the interior of the home, you should always select products that have low to zero volatile organic compounds (VOCs). Thanks to the demand in the market for safe products and materials, and industry standard labeling practices, all you have to do is look at the label to learn a product's safety profile.

Paint for good health

I cannot prove this, but professional painters who have been in the business a long time always seem to struggle with a number of health problems. Some I have known have even seemed to be just a bit off-center, if you know what I mean. This is not a character judgment—there is a medical reason at play. In the past, paints and stains have been so dangerous that they have caused brain damage in a number of veteran painters. Volatile fumes in paint are released when it is applied, and they not only effect painters, but can become part of a persistent toxic mix in homes that affect you and your family.

Thanks to the green movement, there is a higher demand for paints that have low to zero VOCs. The chemicals referred to as VOCs don't necessarily create the smell of paint when it is applied, but rather, are what the paint off-gases throughout its lifecycle. Oil-based paints are the paints that "stink" when they are applied. Acrylic or water-based paints, are the paints with low to zero VOC options. Painters will notice little difference between low to zero VOC "green" paints and other water-based paints. Painters who are used to painting oil-based paints will find that acrylic paints require at least two coats, and can appear thin in nature when painting in darker colors.

When I hired a new painting company to help us on our Hybrid Homes, I asked the owner what he thought of the low-VOC paint they were applying. He said that he would never paint with the other paints again, because he could tell the difference in how his head felt at the end of the day. He said that if he noticed that in one day, imagine how homeowners would feel after years in the home."

Exactly!

New houses used to smell like new cars because of all of the paints, adhesives and other materials used. I enjoy watching homeowners' reaction when they walk into their finished hybrid homes and do not smell anything. They are a bit taken back because they think

Social Media Callout Box

(Post the sentence below to your social media account.)

I like the house to smell and feel like a set of clean sheets that have been on the clothesline all day.

a new house is supposed to smell a certain way. I like the house to smell and feel like a set of clean sheets that have been on the clothesline all day. (If you don't know what that smells like, try it sometime—you have never smelled or felt anything so fresh!)

Finishes on cabinets and other furniture should be low to zero VOC to prevent off-gassing. Recent reports indicate most cabinet makers, big and small, are switching to water-based stains and clear coat finishes, offering a greener product line. Believe it or not, even the Amish cabinet makers we have used on a few of our projects have moved to using water-based finishes on their cabinets! The benefits of low-VOC finishes around the house are many, and the less off-gassing a home experiences, the better its inhabitants will feel.

Everyone is aware of the dangers of lead-based paint in older homes. Many states now require contractors to be licensed to remove leaded paint when remodeling a home. Landlords must verify that they do not have lead-based paint in their rental units, and can be liable for associated health problems if they do. While lead-based paints are no longer on the market, you should be very careful when it comes to sanding or removing old paint. Lead is toxic to touch and breath, so if you have any doubt as to what kind of paint you are about to tamper with, be sure to call in a licensed contractor to check it out before you proceed any further!

Interior building materials

The environmental impact of the materials and products you select for inside your home should always be at the forefront of your mind. As I mentioned at the beginning of this chapter, bamboo was once thought of as *the* green product. It didn't take long before people learned of the negative impact bamboo product manufacturing had on the environment. Still, people with concerns about the environment question the use of pine lumber because pine trees used in lumber and other building products can require over thirty years of growth before harvest.

Social Media Callout Box
(Post the sentence below to your social media account.)

It didn't take long before people learned of the negative impact bamboo product had on the environment.

Thankfully, the lumber industry is trying to do a better job of harvesting their product responsibly. The Forestry Stewardship Council (FSC) developed a certification process that ensures lumber is properly harvested. On a recent trip to Washington State, I got to see this forestation process in action. All the forests were marked to indicate when they were harvested, re-planted, and when they would be harvested again. When lumberjacks cut lumber, FSC certified or not, entire mountains are clear cut, and only rock and dirt are left. It is a terrible thing to see in person, whether or not you are passionate about the environment like me. Lumber and products that carry the FSC certification cost more than normal lumber, and many question if the FSC stamp is worth it. Any attempt to lessen the load on the planet is worth it, but there are alternatives to FSC-certified woods.

One alternative to FSC-certified wood is finger-jointed lumber. Finger-jointed lumber uses several smaller pieces of wood to make a full length piece of lumber. Finger-jointed 2x4 and 2x6 walls studs are a great example of this technology. Manufacturers have started to use finger-jointed lumber in their products. Andersen Windows uses finger-jointed lumber in the manufacturing of a number of their window and door units; they even have a machine that directs all of the scraps created during manufacturing to finger-jointing machines, so nothing is wasted.

(www.hexitherm.com)

In fact, one of the best things your builder can do is to save and recycle all wood scraps from the building project. Throwing out lumber that is over one foot in length is wrong, in my opinion; those leftover pieces of lumber can be used in a house for something useful. If you want to validate the claims of a builder you are interviewing, stop by one of their jobsites and look in the dumpster. One look, and you will see whether or not they walk their talk. If you go to a jobsite and there is no dumpster present while the house is being built, it means the builder is recycling all scrap material rather than sending them to fill up a landfill.

That's the kind of builder you want!

What's in a floor?

A question I am frequently asked is, "What other choices are there besides bamboo for flooring in a house?" First off, there are safe products made of bamboo that are currently on the market, so not all bamboo is bad. Besides bamboo, there are other wood flooring options that are friendly to the environment that are now available to the general public. Other than the harvesting and growing practices of a product, proximity to a jobsite is something that should be considered. Bamboo, for example, grows very quickly, but comes from China across the ocean on ships. The amount of fuel it takes to get bamboo to a jobsite from China should be considered. I'm not trying to pick on bamboo—it's just a good example of how a "green" product can still cause environmental problems.

Acceptable alternatives to bamboo are woods that are considered locally grown, such as oak or maples. One good option for determining what is green and not-so-green is a green building certification program. The United States Green Building Council's LEED for Homes program ensures a house is being built "green." A program like LEED for Homes will take a homeowner and builder step-by-step through the building process, assigning points for green features on a home. Once the points are tallied, homes are given a rating, which range from certified to platinum, with platinum being the highest. There is an entire section in the LEED for Homes process on acceptable building materials, which is an excellent guide for determining if the components of a home are green, and more importantly, safe for you and the environment

Besides wood floors, there are other options for flooring. These options include certain tiles and marmoleum, which are considered green. Using recycled or reused wood is always favorable. And I have seen incredible stained concrete work that looks great inside a house.

Decide what you like, then look for the product that fulfills your desires. With technology and the demand in the market, chances are, you no longer have to completely change your wants and needs because of the availability of a product or material. The days of living with an unattractive feature because it is environmentally friendly are over.

How many light bulbs does it take to change an electric bill?

When was the last time you looked at your electric bill to see how many kilowatt hours of power you used over the past month? Did you know that most electric companies provide that information on your bill, and also disclose your average daily electrical use? This information is important, especially if you are looking to conserve electricity by buying any one of the numerous products available on the market today.

Do you know what the watt rating on a light bulb really means? I didn't until someone explained it to me. Let's use a 100-watt incandescent light bulb, because the math is easier to understand and calculate. Now, on your electric bill, your electrical usage is in kilowatt hours or kWh, and you pay based on how many kWh you use in a particular month. A 100-watt incandescent light bulb will use 100 watts or .1 kWH if it is left on for one hour continuously. Let's say you left that light on for 24 hours straight; that light bulb would use 2.4 kWh of electricity. After averaging electricity bills from numerous people, I have determined a good, working average of daily electricity use is about 19 kWh of power. If the average daily usage of electricity from all of those homes is 19 kWh, then one 100-watt light bulb left on for 24 hours straight would equal just over twelve percent of the daily electrical use in an average home.

Basically the same holds true for appliances and anything else that has a watt rating. By calculating how many kWh a houses uses or will use, we can determine how efficient the house will be before we even build it. One of the most important things I do when I meet with clients as we get ready to design and build their new house is ask to see their electric bill in their current home. The electric bill gives me a valuable look at how they use their electricity. Whether they use renewable energy or not on their new home, I can determine how to lower the electrical consumption by understanding their electric usage and habits. Before you buy anything to conserve electricity, be sure to understand how you are currently using electricity; from there you can lower your bill by controlling your consumption. It's no different than learning what gas mileage your vehicle gets!

Later on we'll look at practical ways to use renewable energy—wind generation, solar panels, etc.—but for now let's consider the products in a home that actually *use* electrical energy. Perhaps the easiest way to reduce the amount of electricity you use is to switch from conventional incandescent light bulbs to energy efficient lighting, such as the CFL light bulb. These inexpensive spiral-shaped bulbs use seventy-five percent less electricity than an incandescent bulb, and give off less heat.

The next best way to conserve electricity in a home is pretty simple: don't leave stuff on! When you leave a room, turn the lights off. If you're not using your computer, shut it off. Habits use more electricity than any appliance or light bulb, so a good way to use less energy is exercise a little discipline.

Thankfully, if you are having a hard time breaking old habits, you can turn to technology for help: install motion sensors in rooms, bathrooms, and any other area that receives a fair amount of traffic. Motion sensors control the lights, not people, and motion sensors can save an incredible amount of energy (and reduce light switch enforcement stress).

I firmly believe that the design and layout of a house can save electricity. A passive solar house is designed to be heated and cooled by the sun and the overhangs of a home, but also to light the most widely used areas of the home. Passive solar will be covered in great detail in the renewable energy chapter of this book. I will explain how you can save energy costs without spending a penny more on your building budget—something you definitely don't want to miss!

Plumbing and the environment

I keep saying it, but it is true: sustainability has everything to do with controlling consumption! Water usage in a home can be astounding. Taking a twenty minute shower uses more water than taking a bath. Most Americans take showers instead of baths, and they take showers on a daily basis. A twenty minute shower with an average shower head can use up to 350 gallons of water per week! While the cost is not incredible for this amount of water usage, the damage on the environment and water table is an inconceivable cost.

Social Media Callout Box

*(Post the sentence below
to your social media account.)*

***Taking a twenty minute
shower uses more water
than taking a bath.***

I have noticed communities rally to fight companies that use ground water to sell for profit as bottled water. Why don't I see those same people come together to conserve water in their own homes? The answer is, because we live in a world where we can flip a switch or valve when we want something and it is always there. What would happen if someday you turned on your shower valve and nothing came out?

My point in all of this is to raise awareness of consumption. To use less water, there are several options. One of these options, using less water while showering, requires a change in habits. Because most people, including myself, have problems changing their habits, the best solution to use less water is to get water-efficient/low-flow water fixtures. As you can imagine, I have heard a lot of comments when I talk about shower-based water conservation in public: "I am not going to stand under a dribble when I take a shower just to save a bucket full of water!" I usually respond by saying, "I don't blame you, but would you use a low-flow shower head if you could have the same pressure as you do now, or better?"

Since you were brave enough to answer the question above and think outside of the box for most of this chapter, I am going to tell you how we have been able to gain better water pressure while using low-flow water fixtures in the new houses that we build. I learned this trick originally from a homeowner who I worked alongside while building his hybrid house. He had a theory that he could increase water pressure in his low-flow fixtures by being conscious of how the supply lines were run to each and every water fixture, including toilets, shower heads, and faucets. The homeowner mentioned that each elbow and connection point in a water line reduces water pressure, and by the time water reaches low-flow fixtures, the pressure is lower than it should be, thus the "dribble effect." To counter this, we used PEX tubing, and bought it in large rolls so we could run one continuous supply line to each water fixture. Too many plumbers use elbows and 'T' connections when running PEX in a house, and the flow of water decreases at each one of these connections. Use one continuous piece of PEX that connects to the water fixture and runs back to a manifold, and the water pressure to that fixture is incredible!

The next trick is to make sure you run a big enough supply line to the manifolds where the continuous runs of PEX connect. We found that using 1-inch inside diameter copper pipe is the best fit for that system. Amazingly, with this system, you can take a shower with a low-flow shower head and actually get soaked! The cost is not any more expensive than if the plumbers ran PEX in the normal fashion. In fact, with the elimination of connections and the time required to seal them, this should be a less-expensive solution. Ask your plumber if they can do this in your new house or remodel and you will not be sorry!

Low-flow water fixtures are available from all major manufacturers of plumbing components. As the name implies, low-flow water fixtures use less water. A twenty minute shower uses half as much water when delivered from a low-flow shower head. The prices for low-flow water fixtures are comparable to regular-flow water fixtures at the big box stores. I have a low-flow water shower head in my shower at home. It is connected to a plumbing system that dates back to the 1950s, when the house was built, and aside for some mineral deposits that have closed a few of the holes up, the pressure is comparable to all of the places I stay during my travels.

The LEED for Homes Program is a great guide to determine whether or not your prospective water fixtures are low-flow. To score the highest points under their green rating program, and have the most energy efficient water fixtures, the following values would apply:

- The average flow rate for all lavatory faucets must be less than or equal to 1.5 gallons per minute (GPM).
- The average flow rate for all shower heads must be less than or equal to 1.75 gallons per minute (GPM).
- The average flow rate for all toilets must be less than or equal to 1.1 gallons per minute (GPM).

Believe or not, toilets have come a long way. Low-flow toilets were notorious for not being able to handle their duties, but today the technology has advanced. Along with low-flow single-flush toilets there's a new type of toilet, the dual-flush toilet. These dual-flush toilets are designed to use little water for liquids and much less water (compared to normal toilets) for solids. Prices of these low-flow toilets compare to regular-flow rate toilets, and are being used by more and more people every day. The only concern that I've heard from a plumber with a low-flow toilet relates to larger houses or septic systems where the drain pipes travel a long distance and have multiple ninety-degree turns. The plumber was worried that the solids may only go so far and then sit there until another flush is made. I agreed that this is a concern, but we have not had any trouble with this phenomenon, knock on wood.

The one thing to glean from this chapter and apply in your own lives is the idea that sustainability has everything to do with controlling consumption. If you don't like high prices at the pump, look for ways to reduce your gas consumption, like carpooling or buying a car with better fuel efficiency. Educated consumption is the key to living a sustainable lifestyle. Once you can wrench yourself free from the wasteful lifestyle of modern society, you will notice a new found love for things like clotheslines, home gardens, and entertaining people at home.

Now it's time to take a closer look at the most popular building systems for residential house construction. If you or someone you know is planning on having a new home built in the future—or if you are a home builder yourself—you'll want to pay attention. I want you to learn what I have learned to save more than just money; it is my hope that reading about why people build and live this way will help you live a more sustainable, rewarding life!

5 INSULATED CONCRETE FORMS

(**NOTE**: In the next four chapters you will see a set of meters that illustrate how each of the four advanced technologies compare to a traditional stick-built house. I've included these meters below. The set of meters on top are for an Insulated Concrete Form (ICF) house, the bottom set of meters are for a traditional stick-built house, and both cover the areas of difficulty, tradition, expense, and energy efficiency.)

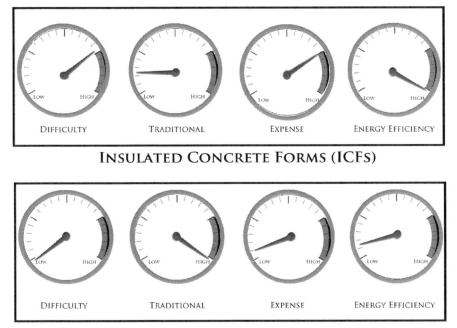

INSULATED CONCRETE FORMS (ICFS)

TRADITIONAL STICK BUILT HOUSE

For the longest time, my cell phone screen read "ICF Man," because when I started my own company, I believed that using ICFs was the best form of construction. I used to have debates with other builders about the merits of their building materials compared to ICFs. I felt so strongly about ICFs, because I knew from experience how well houses built with ICFs could perform.

Insulated Concrete Forms are exactly as the name implies: an insulated, stay-in-place concrete form. ICFs are stacked on top of each other and are used for building basement and main floor walls. When installed and properly braced, ICFs are poured with concrete and the forms are not removed. The forms insulate both the exterior and interior of a wall, and unlike conventional stick-framed walls, offer continuous insulation for the entire length of a wall.

My love affair with ICFs began in the early 1990s, but ICFs date back much further. In-fact, in the early1960s, a Swiss company named Agrisol marketed the first insulated concrete form. This would lead to several patents and a slew of competition. In just over forty years, the ICF industry has grown from one manufacturer to more than sixty, with the bulk of this growth occurring over the last decade. There is no doubt that the interest in using ICFs in building has soared. I've noticed that big box stores have ICFs for sale; if the big box stores are trying to sell ICFs, then there is definitely considerable interest.

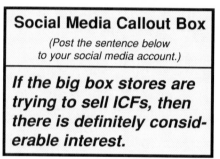

Social Media Callout Box
*(Post the sentence below
to your social media account.)*

If the big box stores are trying to sell ICFs, then there is definitely considerable interest.

There are three ICF cavity configurations: flat wall, waffle grid, and screen grid. Flat wall is by far the more popular choice with the architects and builders that I am aware of, because there is no special engineering required (unlike the waffle grid and screen grid ICFs). Flat wall is just that—a uniformed flat wall inside the ICF which has the same thickness over the entire ICF wall. This style of ICF is the style that we use on our ICF projects. Back in the early 1990s, we used the waffle grid style of ICF, and the ICFs available on the market were also waffle grid.

Waffle grid ICFs have horizontal and vertical cores with thinner areas of concrete between these cores. If the foam were stripped away from the wall, you would see something that resembles a waffle. It is up to the installer to line up the cores to build the strength in this wall configuration. A waffle grid ICF wall uses about twenty five percent less concrete than a flat wall. Screen grid is similar to the waffle grid, but requires an onsite installer to install splines in the wall system to attach the system together. It has been my experience that flat wall ICFs are easier to use, and produce a better end product than the other two forms of ICFs.

The United States Department of Housing and Urban Development, along with the National Association of Home Builders, created a manual for ICFs called the *"Prescriptive Method For Insulating Concrete Forms In Residential Construction."* Successful ICF builders keep several copies of this manual on hand to assuage any discomfort felt by building inspectors. It is always a great idea to give a copy of this book to the building inspector if you are building with ICFs–this is a secret of veteran ICF builders. The *Prescriptive Method* contains all the information a person or inspector would need to assemble an ICF wall and ensure the best possible strength profile. If the building inspector has never inspected a house made of ICFs, then *Prescriptive Method* will be worth its weight in gold.

Most ICFs that are on the market today are made of expanded polystyrene (EPS), the foam with little beads in it. EPS does not use chlorofluorocarbons (CFCs) in its production, which are harmful to the environment. The main reason why most ICFs are made with EPS is because EPS is more durable than extruded polystyrene. Extruded polystyrene is very brittle and does not hold up well on jobsites.

The majority of the ICFs on the market are forty-eight inches long and sixteen inches high, however, there are larger ICFs available. Most ICF brands are the same size because they are all molded at the same facilities. Changing the length of the ICF would cost more money, so most manufactures sell the standard forty-eight inch by sixteen inch form. The most important part of the ICF is not the size, but rather, the nailing flanges and how they are assembled. Nailing flanges are built into the ICF and create the platform for fastening siding, drywall, and anything else that is to be used on an ICF home.

Another important consideration is how the corner ICF is designed. In the ICF industry, very few manufacturers have a corner ICF that will work equally well with the numerous types of siding that are on the market. (I tried for years to try to get an ICF company to respond to this concern, but to no avail.) Nailing or screwing five and a half inch exterior trim boards will not work on the majority of the ICF corners available on the market today. Most forms need to be hot knifed out, and have a half inch of plywood fastened to the corners to keep the exterior corner trim from curling and falling off. The same holds true for vinyl siding corners. When making decisions on a specific ICF, look first at the corner ICF and see where and if the corner has a nailing flange. While studies show that ICF homes cost more to build, most overages in price are due to the learning curve. My best advice: match the ICF that you use to type of exterior finish that you will have on your house.

When selecting an ICF, price should not be a primary deciding factor. A more expensive ICF can actually save you money because

---

Social Media Callout Box

(Post the sentence below to your social media account.)

A more expensive ICF can actually save you money.

---

in most cases it will reduce costs in installation labor, including siding, dry walling, and trimming. One must think about all of the money saved by reducing labor costs on all of these areas when making an ICF purchase. I have used the most expensive ICFs on the market, but I can tell you from experience, these expensive forms are worth it!

ICFs and your building site

Most building sites are suitable for ICF use, but some building site adjustment may be needed, and that can add costs to a project. The following questions can help you determine *before* the design phase of a home if ICFs are going to fit the budget of a project. Unforeseen challenges add costs to a project that homeowners and/or builders have not considered. I have learned the hard way to ask these questions and use the answers to guide us to the appropriate form of construction based on the conditions at the building site.

What type of soil does the building site have and will this soil support the weight of a home built with ICFs? First point to consider is the type of soil and the water table height. If a building site is near a lake for instance, the soil may not be suitable for the weight of an-all concrete home. Always consult with a soil engineer before starting a project if there is any question about soil type.

We once built a house very close to a lake, and the original design prescribed ICFs. Once we looked at the building site and saw that two springs came out of the ground very near to where the house would be built, we brought in a soil engineer. The engineer helped us determine than an all-ICF house was too heavy for the building site, because the springs actually flowed beneath the house. Had we not brought in a soil engineer, we would have had a serious problem, as the house would have settled more than normal.

Is there good access to the building site and can large concrete trucks work in the building area? Assuming the site will support an all-ICF home, next assess if there is adequate access to the building site for all of the heavy equipment that is required to install ICFs. Building in an open field is the perfect situation for pouring ICFs because equipment can move around without any obstructions. The concrete pump truck is an enormous vehicle that needs room to set up and rotate. Concrete trucks pull up behind the concrete pump truck, so there needs to be enough room for these trucks to line up. Building in an extremely wooded area with a winding driveway, for example, could cause access issues and drive an overrun in price due to equipment charges or towing fees. Being proactive and recognizing potential obstructions *before* you break ground for construction can save you and your builder a fair amount of money.

I always dreaded Mondays, not because I love my weekends, but because that is when all the crazy phone calls would come in. Once we built a house on the back side of a big field and the access was supposedly an old road. I assumed that the old road was like other roads and had a gravel base, which would adequately support the larger equipment. One Monday morning, I answered my phone and all I could hear were big diesel engines running in the background.

It had snowed a few inches during the night and apparently a concrete truck, full of concrete, was stuck on that access road. I asked them to text me a picture of what was going on, and when I looked at the picture they sent me, I gasped! Stuck in the field at the bottom of a hill were two fully loaded concrete trucks, a massive concrete pump truck, and a bull dozer. They were all strapped together and stuck up to their axles. Talk about losing money before the job even started! After that day, I now insist that clients have a good gravel-based drive put in before we even begin construction, and I definitely recommend anyone reading this book to do the same.

Are there any overhead obstructions that could prevent a concrete pump truck from fully extending in to the air? Have you ever been to a big city and seen someone looking up in the air, then, all of the sudden, everyone is looking up in the air? The old *Superman* television show comes to mind. Well, that is exactly what you should do when you are standing on your building site. Looking for overhead obstructions is every bit as important as calling MISS DIG to look for underground obstructions.

The boom on a concrete pump truck can be over fifty feet tall, and if there is not adequate clearance on the site, extra costs may rack up for the added time it will take to reposition the pump truck. If you are building in a city or neighborhood, be very conscious of the weight of these vehicles, and the overhead obstructions that exist on every city or neighborhood street.

Concrete pump trucks charge by the hour and they usually start charging when they leave their place of business. All the concrete pump truck should ever do is pump concrete—every reposition costs money. Each time you scratch your head, deciding how to get the pump truck into a workable position at your building site, you are losing lots of money! Be proactive and have a plan in place before you even begin construction; if you do this, you will save money.

Do you have a back-up plan on site in case one of the concrete trucks get stuck? There is no doubt that there is a perfect time of year, no matter what the location, to build a project—a time of year when the drive into a project is not muddy or icy or snow covered. In a perfect world, you would start building a home

73

in the late spring and complete the project before late fall. Consider the extra costs of building at non-optimum times of the year in your area. If a person is starting a project during the winter in the Midwest, then they should know what they are getting themselves into. It is always a great idea to have a bulldozer on site at all times to clear the driveways and pull out any heavy trucks that get stuck. The cost of hiring tow trucks to pull large vehicles out of bad areas and the down time it costs the project can amount to thousands of dollars.

Some builders will have miscellaneous funds built into the project budget to cover these unforeseen challenges, and some builders gladly pass these additional costs down to the homeowners. The same situations can occur in the spring and fall in the Midwest, depending on where the jobsite is at. If it has been raining, building in an old farm field is one of the toughest spots. Be sure that there is a piece of equipment on site before the problem arises, and be sure to read the subcontractors contracts very clearly. Most of those contracts will state that there needs to be a clear path in and out of the jobsite, and that if any equipment gets stuck, it is the homeowners responsibility to pay for the towing costs.

Here's a trick I learned: look for a local small time excavator in the vicinity of the build. I always ask the homeowner if they know anyone who might have a bulldozer, and in most instances, they do. I would meet the excavator out at the jobsite and ask them if they could leave their dozer on the site, and most times, they would, especially since the majority of the work that requires the big concrete trucks happens before the foundation is backfilled. We saved thousands of dollars by having a dozer on site, ready to pull out trucks that got stuck, because I believed that a vehicle getting stuck was never an *if* but a *when*.

Is there a place for the concrete pump truck and the concrete trucks to clean out? Clean out is messy and leaves a large pile of concrete that hardens and becomes very difficult to move. I remember several jobsites where we were building on a lake and were constantly inspected by the Environmental Protection Agency (EPA). Can you imagine the look on an EPA inspector's face if they saw a concrete truck spilling concrete and contaminated water on the beach? Whether you are building on a lake or building in a subdivision, you can save a lot of hassle by determining ahead of time what to do with the excess concrete that is washed out of the concrete truck.

Most times, ICF installers order an extra half-yard of concrete to make up for what they lose during the clean out of the concrete pump truck and the priming of the pump. Most of that half-yard of concrete is dropped straight out of the bottom of the pump truck hopper into a large pile. If this clean out occurs on a project site that has very little room to maneuver on, the clean out pile can be an expensive obstacle to overcome. As soon as that pile of concrete hardens, only a large piece of equipment can move it. We always kept pieces of rebar on hand that we bent like a handle. We put these rebar pieces in the wet concrete, creating a chain hook point when the pile of concrete hardened. We could then move the pile of concrete out of the way without it being too much of a hassle.

Some excavators can be sweet talked into removing the concrete pieces when they work on excavation work on the site. Never toss these concrete chunks in the jobsite dumpster because that can cost you added money; most dumpster companies charge extra for putting concrete in their dumpsters. Ask a contractor or subcontractor how they are going to handle the waste concrete and this could save a big hassle or cost at some point during the project.

Have you considered the delivery of building products and materials to your site? A jobsite doesn't have to be in a remote or secluded area to present difficulties when it comes to the delivery of products and materials. I once tried to do a favor for one of our sub-contractors by meeting a truck driver at a jobsite. I was going to help the truck driver unload a semi-truck full of ICFs. As I approached the jobsite, I could see a semi parked in the roadway, causing a traffic jam. When I walked up to the truck driver, he said "All I do is drive, I don't unload." I was there by myself, and the bundles of ICFs were 8 feet long! Luckily a couple of locals showed up and helped me for $20 and a case of beer each. It was one of the most dangerous things I have ever done, because the semi was parked on a busy road at the crest of a hill.

Social Media Callout Box

(Post the sentence below to your social media account.)

Be sure that if you are going to use ICFs, you have a safe place to unload them.

Be sure that if you are going to use ICFs, you have a safe place to unload them. ICFs in most cases are directly shipped to the jobsite from the manufacturer. This means that the ICFs are shipped on over-the-road semi trailers and packaged to fit as many ICFs into a trailer as possible. This has been one of the biggest complaints in the ICF industry, because each ICF brand is package differently. I would always insist that our ICFs were shipped in small cubes so they could be handled by one person. For a while, I only bought the most expensive ICFs because they were shipped in the safest manner. It is a good idea to ask your salesperson how the ICFs will show up.

Since most ICFs are shipped in semi trucks, typically, drivers do not or cannot help with the unloading. This means that if a semi shows up on the crest of a hill during the middle part of the day, the unloading of the truck can be quite dangerous and difficult. Semis cannot leave the roadway and pull into driveways or onto some dirt roads because the trucks are not designed to do that. Be sure to have a truck, trailer, and a few people to help unload the semi, and this will help create a positive experience with ICFs from the very start of the project.

Architects and building plans

Now that a homeowner and/or builder has determined that the project site is a good fit for ICFs, it is time to get the architect or designer involved. Sometimes the only difference between an architect and a designer is the length of time they went to school and the required licensing. Some designers are really good at drawing pictures and have no clue about structural issues. In these cases, the designer will pay an architect to review their drawings. This is the case for ICF homes, especially if the designer is new to drawing structures that will incorporate ICFs.

Like selecting a contractor or subcontractor, finding a designer or architect with ICF experience is the key to keeping a project on budget. A good to great set of plans can save money, even if the plans cost more to produce. The reason is, onsite workers can be more efficient with a set of building plans that includes provisions to answer every possible question. Time is money, and someone using ICFs should insist on having a very detailed set of prints on site. This should hold true for all forms of building, but especially so when building with ICFs.

ICFs added a new twist to the world of building. Now, workers who normally install traditionally poured walls and poured driveways are building the exterior walls of a home. Using a detailed set of plans will ensure that no problems arise later in the project. I always insisted that a set of building plans have multiple dimensions to keep onsite workers from guessing at measurements. Trimming out a house or placing a stairway in an opening that was built incorrectly because someone onsite made an inaccurate guess at a measurement is a problem that is not easily fixed. Leading ICF builders insist on having as many dimensions and details as possible on the prints to prevent errors that occur when people guess off of a low-detail set of prints. This means that the designer or architect must be very good at what they do, because they ultimately are responsible for any problems that arise as a result of an error on their part. The building team should always review the prints for errors before any work is done on the project, and never assume that the designer or architect was error-free in drawing the plans.

If possible, avoid using plans that were not designed from the beginning to use ICFs. The difference in wall thickness between conventional homes and ICF homes can cause major problems in the house's layout. Houses that have powder rooms or hallways located on exterior walls will consequently be smaller in dimension, and that can mean that doors providing passage into such rooms will not open all the way up. It's more cost effective to have an architect create a design that takes into count the wall thickness of an ICF home.

Additionally, the architect should design the project to the specific brand ICF that will be used on the project. This means assessing whether wall dimensions work with not only the length of the straight blocks, but with the corner blocks as well. With a little thought, the designer or architect can make a wall dimension that will equal a convenient number of whole blocks, eliminating extra cutting and labor to install the ICFs. This simple step will reduce labor costs in the project. Moreover, the ICF will take less time to install when a wall is drawn properly, Creating additional cost savings. These considerations will reduce the overall cost of building an ICF home.

Another area of an ICF house to pay attention to is a "bump out." A room should never stick out less than the length of the ICF corner block, because the corner strength of the building and ICF are compromised every time an ICF is cut. Windows that are installed in the side walls of these bump-out areas should have enough ICF remaining between the window and the corner so that the corner can be braced properly. All major ICF brands come with architect CAD drawings, so adapting a specific ICF to a project is no more labor intensive than installing the CD or DVD that the manufacturer supplies. Designing a project to a specific ICF can reduce waste by an incredible amount!

Plan ahead with concrete

The most important thing to remember when working with concrete is that once the concrete sets up, making changes is nearly impossible without incurring incredible expense. I always work with the architect or designer to make notes of any and all "pass-throughs" on the building plans and ensure that no pass-throughs get missed on the concrete wall. Pass-throughs are areas of the ICF wall that have pipes or other items pass through the ICF wall. An example of a pass-through would be ventilation pipes for the air exchanger in the home. Air exchanger pass-throughs are more than seven inches in circumference for each pipe. If this seven-plus-inch hole were forgotten, cutting a hole through the reinforced concrete could take several hours. There are several pass-throughs on an average house; be sure to check with all of the sub-contractors on a project to verify that none of the pass-throughs are passed up.

Electrical plans are another key component of efficient ICF-build planning. Not all architects and designers offer to draw the electrical plans for a home. A set of electrical plans can also be sketched up by the electrician on a project if they are not part of the building plans. It's important to have electrical plans on an ICF project because the ICF installers can install any pass-through required for the electrical system. Also, if asked or required, many ICF installers will install electrical conduit and electrical boxes in the ICF walls before they pour the concrete. There are other benefits to having a usable electrical plan with the set of building plans, the most important being that it aligns the entire building team for the entire length of the project.

Once a person has decided on the right ICF based on the needs of their home design, it's time to prepare to install the ICFs or find a qualified ICF installer. If you are a homeowner and choose to install the ICFs yourself, then pay *incredible* attention to detail during installation. Once the concrete is set up, it is next to impossible to fix any errors due to an improper install. The installer must make sure that the forms are fastened to the footings, so the bottom of the forms do not move when the ICFs are poured with concrete. Always follow the instructions of the ICF brand you are using. If you have any questions or concerns with the installation of ICFs, your ICF salesperson will gladly help you answer them.

Even if you plan on building your home yourself, I always recommend that do-it-yourselfers hire a qualified ICF installer. Once a do-it-yourselfer figures in the cost of bracing, the ICFs, and everything associated with ICF installation, hiring an ICF installer makes great sense. There are several areas of a home where doing it yourself can create overall cost savings. ICFs, however, are best left to professional installers who will make sure that the ICFs are straight and plumb. It's not that I don't believe that you can do it; it's that I know that having a qualified ICF installer do your ICF work is worth it!

When ICFs arrive at a jobsite, the most widely used brands will be packaged one of two ways. The first and most popular way is in the form of a four-foot cube. These cubes are easy to handle and they store well on a jobsite. The other way that ICFs arrive is in an eight-foot-tall stack. This unruly eight-foot-tall stack requires a few people to handle, and if the delivery semi parks out on the edge of the property, a truck and/or trailer will be required to get the ICF stacks to the actual jobsite.

vs.

If you still insist on installing the ICFs yourself, let me give you a little advice: bracing is the key to a successful ICF installation.

Without proper bracing, ICFs can fall down and will end up out of level and plumb. Walls that are out of level and plumb can cause major problems, especially when it comes to installing kitchen cabinets and windows and doors. A qualified ICF installer will have everything they need to brace the ICFs properly. Bracing window and door "bucks" so they remain flush with the ICFs and level and plumb is critical to a clean, professional finished look. A window buck is made of wood, PVC, or metal, and is what windows and doors attached to in an ICF wall.

Time to decide

There are many advantages to using ICFs in a residential project. ICFs provide a continuous insulation with very limited air infiltration. When combined with passive solar design and/or a geothermal system, ICFs help to keep heating and cooling costs down by providing superior insulation to a conventional stick-framed wall. ICFs can withstand wind speeds up to 300 mph, making the house a very safe, sturdy structure. A house built with ICFs is nearly soundproof, making for a comfortable, warm, quiet, and enjoyable home. Using ICFs can help to eliminate construction waste and decrease labor cost by making the building process more efficient compared to conventional framing.

ICFs do have disadvantages, one of them being the lack of qualified installers. ICFs are only as good as those installing them and those manufacturing them. There are close to 100 brands of ICFs and less than 10 of those brands would be considered by industry experts as acceptable for building. ICFs that are not manufactured properly are prone to "blow outs," which is when the Styrofoam breaks while pouring concrete into the ICF, causing the concrete to blow out. Improper ICF installation can cause walls to be out of plumb and unleveled; this causes unforeseen problems later in the building process. Building a custom home out of ICFs takes skill. If an ICF wall is out of plumb where cabinets will be hung, it is very difficult to get the cabinets to fit to the wall and look good; this is a major disadvantage to using ICFs.

Cost can also be seen as a disadvantage to using ICFs. Typically, an ICF home costs ten percent more to build than a home without ICFs. This is a major disadvantage to those not well versed in ICF construction, but does not matter as much to those who already plan to build with ICFs. Sub-contractors can be unsure of how to price a job that is made of ICFs. Constantly educating sub-contractors and inspectors about ICFs and how to work with them can be a disadvantage.

Overall, an ICF home will provide great energy savings that will offset the increase costs of building this type of structure. A professional builder who has built several ICF homes is your best bet since he will have found ways to work around some of the inherent issues that a do-it-yourselfer might miss. Before you decide, consider the next type of building method.

6 STRUCTURAL INSULATED PANELS (SIPs)

Overall, I have found SIPs to be the best value for the dollar, which is saying a lot because I've done so much work with ICFs. I

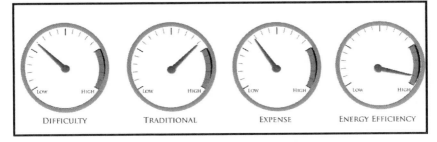

STRUCTURAL INSULATED PANELS (SIPs)

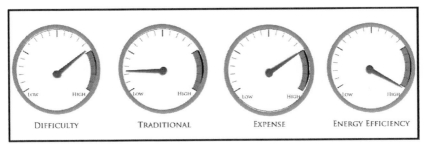

INSULATED CONCRETE FORMS (ICFs)

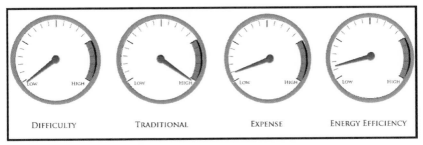

TRADITIONAL STICK BUILT HOUSE

discovered that using SIPs can produce a house similar in tightness to an ICF house while keeping the price down. If you look at the meters below, which are based on all of the different types of houses that we have built, you can see right away that the SIP house is less difficult to build than an ICF house, and is almost as energy efficient. This is incredible news, because achieving that level of energy efficiency used to cost so much more!

SIPs have been around for many years, and have been used in different parts of the country. SIPs have wood panels on both sides with foam sandwiched in between the wood. SIPs originated in Wisconsin, and the original concept was first considered around 1935. Frank Lloyd Wright, a progressive architect in his time, used SIPs in a few of his affordable homes around the 1940s.

Alden B. Dow of the Dow Chemical family in Midland, Michigan, is credited as the creator of the first foam-core SIP. That creation fueled increased usage of these foam-core SIPs, because it made the installation process much more efficient and affordable. I remember watching a SIP house being built near my hometown as a kid in the late 1980s. I really liked how different it was from the other stick-framed houses. I never knew what that house was made of until I started researching SIPs for use on our first SIP-built house.

With the recent growth of green building, more and more people are interested in using SIPs for the exterior envelope of their homes. In my experience, SIPs are without a doubt the best value when it comes to tight exterior envelopes. If you are looking for a home that is almost as airtight

Social Media Callout Box
(Post the sentence below to your social media account.)

SIPs are without a doubt the best value when it comes to tight exterior envelopes.

as an ICF house, but costs much less, using SIPs is the way. SIPs can greatly reduce the labor on a project, and this alone lowers the price of a SIP house.

The first time we used SIPs for the exterior walls on a house was when we were forced to. The soil on which we were building could not support the weight of an all-ICF house. Prior to this build, we used SIPs for roofs on some of our projects, and I loved how they performed as part of our system. We built that first SIP house so tough, because we glued everything together and learned along the way *exactly* how to assemble the exterior walls of a SIP house. It was an eye opening experience for me—we put the exterior walls up quicker than if we had framed them like a conventional wall.

SIPs are comparable in air tightness to ICFs, but there are differences between SIPs and ICFs when used in exterior wall construction. A prime reason people desire ICF homes is the incredible strength of the concrete walls. Proponents of ICFs will point out the fact that the very real difference between ICFs and SIPs is the possibility of penetration in the event of a major storm. There are plenty of pictures available of walls or trees after a tornado sent airborne debris through them. This is the one thing that SIPs can't do that ICFs can. Since SIPs are made of foam sandwiched between two pieces of oriented strand board (OSB), the SIP is not capable of stopping penetrations like an ICF can. While it is true that debris can penetrate a SIP wall, the SIP is still tougher than a stick built wall. Airborne debris may penetrate and stick in the SIP wall, but this same debris would pass completely through a conventionally framed wall. SIPs are a great product, that, when installed properly, result in a tough, air tight house.

Those who choose SIPs find an incredible value in building with them. Other than the penetration issue mentioned above, houses built of SIPs and houses built of ICFs share nearly identical results on energy testing. Both forms of construction are very durable, but prospective homeowners who want an airtight home on a tight budget should put their focus on SIPs. You will learn below that there still can be thermal pass-through in a SIP house. Cold air can still transfer at all of the connection points in a house built with SIPs, unless you take steps that help eliminate this thermal pass through.

There are several SIP manufactures around the country and most operate the exact same way: each order is made specifically for each client. Therefore, it is very important for the client to give the SIP manufacturer the final and approved set of building prints. Providing the SIP manufacturer with a preliminary sketch or a set of plans from a magazine without thorough review can be a very costly mistake. Always make sure that the building prints submitted to the manufacturer are the final set, with all corrections and changes made and finalized. Like working with ICFs, SIPs are not easily changed if there is an error. Be sure that all window rough opening sizes are correct and any and all pass-throughs are marked on the prints, so the SIP engineers can approve their placement and sizes.

The SIP manufacturer will take a client's final building prints and make a set of prints to coincide with the SIP panel order. If the client has a set of electrical plans with the building prints, then the SIP manufacturer will usually install whatever outlet and switch openings are listed on the electrical prints. This can save the electricians a lot of grief and labor time, because all the electricians will have to do is "fish" the electrical wires through the premade openings and wire channels. This is something that I really like about SIPs—it eases the stress on the electricians, and helps keep their pricing reasonable.

Most SIP manufacturers create three dimensional (3D) rotating models of the home so that the builder and/or homeowner can see how the SIPs will look when installed. The SIP manufacturer then creates a list of SIP panels and where they go on the home per the finalized building prints from the client. Headers, window and door openings, and any other features that would normally be stick-framed are included in the SIP package. Most SIP headers are insulated so there is minimal thermal pass-through. The SIP manufacturer will give the client a floor plan drawing for each floor of the home that uses SIPs. These floor plans will show the exterior wall of the home and any other wall that will use SIPs. Each SIP will be numbered, and is designed to go in a specific spot in the house. A SIP schedule is provided that shows how each SIP is to be positioned, what it looks like as a single panel, and also how it is to be fastened to the subfloor and to each consecutive panel.

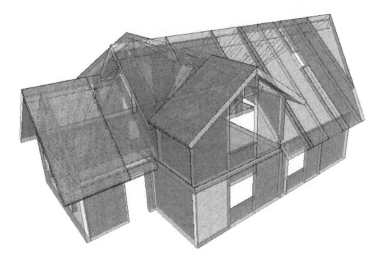

After we built our first SIP house, I decided the only way to make sure the building process would go smoothly was to meet with the SIP manufacturer to verify the SIPs were correct. Our team would verify that the dimensions on the SIP manufacturer's prints matched the dimensions on the final set of the actual building prints. CAD operators enter the wrong numbers, just by error, more often than you might expect. This error can cost a crew an incredible amount of downtime, which can be avoided by a print review in the comfort of an office. I spent whatever time was necessary to verify every single measurement on the SIP prints matched those on the building prints. Every time I did, I found an error! To save money on a project, you must try to limit funds spent on labor; if crews have to correct errors on the jobsite, it costs money! Be proactive and never order anything until you are sure that the order will be correct.

I remember a high profile SIP project we worked on that had a major problem with labeling. The house was the first one we worked on that was designed by cutting edge SIP software, so initially we thought we could leverage this fact as a marketing tool. The problem was that there was a glitch in the software, and once I caught errors in the dimensioning, the software relabeled each SIP that was corrected. This put first floor SIPs in the second floor SIP pile, so delivery was a nightmare, and our installers stood around waiting for SIPs to arrive. It was a costly dilemma. A client should pay close attention to the SIP manufacturer's prints and be absolutely sure that there are no questions or errors on the SIP prints. Ask about how they label their SIPs, especially if there are to be corrections made to the order.

Just as with ICFs, a client should always ask how the SIPs will be delivered to the jobsite. SIPs are always shipped logistically, and that means that the SIPs will not arrive in the order of installation. If the SIP manufacturer uses a flatbed semi-trailer to deliver the SIPs, there must be ample room on the job site to store the SIPs so they can be sorted out and put in the proper order of installation. Most semi drivers will not leave a paved road, and that can be a huge problem for a do-it-yourselfer who is not prepared to unload the SIPs along a roadway. A SkyTrak forklift with long forks is the best bet for unloading the SIPs. I always include a SkyTrak forklift allowance in the budget for SIP houses, and I recommend that you do the same.

Depending on the order size, the SIP load might be sent out on a smaller trailer and sent in several loads. If this is the case, then it is very important not to schedule installation of the SIPs until all of the SIPs are on site—I learned this lesson the hard way. When SIPs are sent in multiple loads, oftentimes the load is missing a few SIPs, based on how the load is stacked on the trailer. To determine how the load will be shipped, just ask the SIP manufacturer; this could prevent costly delays on a project. I would normally have two people on site to unload and stack the SIPs in installation order, once we knew the delivery time.

If there is a crew of more than two on the jobsite, then it is normal to separate into two teams. One team sorts the SIPs and places them in order of installation, while the other team lays out the sub-floor and attaches the plates the SIPS will connect to when they are hoisted and made into a wall. Most SIPs are five and one half inches in thickness, so a 2x6 is used as the plate. If the house is complex, it is a good idea to write the SIP number on the subfloor where the SIP panel will be attached. This will help eliminate errors. Once a panel is glued and nailed or stapled in place, it is very difficult to move the panel without damaging it. Be sure to put each panel in the correct position! I found it valuable to assign one person with the sole task of reading the prints and ensuring the SIPs were installed in the correct spots.

Installing SIPs

A person who has experience framing a conventional stick-framed wall, will have little problem installing SIP panels. Installing SIPs is actually quite simple, and is a welcome change from conventional framing. Once the panel is stood vertical, the wall is done. The wall is already insulated and sheeted, and installing SIPs can progress quickly, which means you can have a house standing and insulated in a day if things go right. The first time I installed SIPs and we completed the first floor walls of a house, I could hardly believe how little time it took.Here's the process I follow in installing SIPs. First and foremost, make sure you review the SIP building prints and 3D drawings in great detail before you begin. The 3D drawings are a great way to see how the panels are supposed to fit together. It is important to read the instruction manual that the SIP manufacturer provides. This manual will give you step-by-step directions on how to install their products safely and properly.

Once you are comfortable with the instruction manual and the layout of the SIPs on the 3D model, you then securely fasten the 2x6 sill plate to the sub-floor (per the SIP manufacturer's fastener schedule). As I pointed out earlier, if you set the panels up in order of how they are to be installed as you unload them from the delivery truck, the next step will go quickly. Remember, the manufacturer recommends that the SIPs are installed according to their specifications. In most cases you can get the SIP sales representative to help you get started with the installation, and I can't recommend this enough if you are a first time SIP user.

We have found that it is important to have enough studs on hand that are the same thickness as the core of the SIPs. This lumber is used for fastening panels together, top and bottom plates, and for making corners. The SIP manufacturers do not supply these studs, and many people mistakenly assume that they do. Once the sill plates are fastened to the sub-floor with adhesive and nails, the installer drills holes in the sill plate and all the way through the sub-floor wherever the corresponding electrical run hole is located on the panel they are installing. This is so the electricians will be able to fish wires through the panels. This simple step can save the electricians an incredible amount of time, and time is money! You can show the electricians what you did to help them out, and this should help to keep their price down.

Before you tip a SIP up and install it, adhesive needs to be applied on the sill plate, per the manufacturer's recommendations. Once the SIP is tilted onto the sill plate and adhesive, then the SIP is fastened to the sill plate with nails or sheathing staples. We found that installing one panel on each side of a corner was a great way to start. We then fastened the two panels together to make a corner. This corner is made plumb in all directions, and then braced to remain plumb and true. Large screws are used to fasten the panels to each other through the corner that is made up of the two panels. From this corner, the rest of the panels are installed.

We learned right away that there is a correct way to position the panel, and that there is an inside, outside, top and bottom to the SIP. The lines on the SIPs indicate where the electrical runs are, and the side of the SIPs with the lines needs to face inward. Without these lines, the electricians have to guess where the electrical runs are, and this takes them extra time, which they charge for! It is vitally important to the entire SIP building system that the holes drilled in the sill plate line up with the holes in the foam core of the SIPs. If the holes match up, then the electrician's job will be a breeze, and if the holes do not line up, you can expect to pay more money to the electricians.

The installation process goes quickly, especially with two teams. One team of two fetches the panels and bracing material and brings them to the installing team, and provides additional assistance outside the home. Always plan a way to carry panels into the house, either by omitting a large panel and installing that panel last or by stacking the needed panels inside the house and on the subfloor. The two-person team that is installing the panels divides their duties as such: one team member glues the sill plates and the connecting lumber, while the other person preps the next panel for installation. Then the two together tilt up panels, fasten, brace, and plumb. If there is a large panel to install, then all four of the installers on site assist in installing that panel.

Installing a SIP roof system is considerably more difficult. SIP roof systems contain a number of very large, very heavy SIP panels that, in most cases, require a crane or a long boomed SkyTrak to set. Without the proper equipment onsite, this can be a costly endeavor for a do-it-yourselfer. If a jobsite has little room for material storage, one method of installing the roof SIPs is to set the SIPs directly from the delivery truck to the roof. This can be a tricky and costly process to coordinate, due to the cost of rental equipment and the tendency for late or delayed SIP deliveries. Be sure to have all required equipment on the jobsite before you ever think of trying to set a SIP roof. The other way that installers approach SIP roof systems is like normal truss installation: the SIPs get delivered, and the crew sets them once the boom truck is scheduled.

Remember that the SIP manufacturer will charge more for beams and large ridge beams than a lumber company will. I learned the hard way that the SIP price does not include the cost of lumber needed to assemble the SIPs or the ridge beam for a SIP roof system. In a house that has a large open span, the ridge beam can cost thousands of dollars, and is not part of the SIP order. I found out how much a ridge beam costs when we needed one at the last minute (no one told me that the ridge beam was not included in the SIP order). It's a good idea to check with your SIP salesperson to see what exactly is included in the price of the order.

Problems with water

Water infiltration always concerned me when working with SIPs. SIPs generally are made using OSB, and OSB does not weather very well. I feel that a leak could destroy the integrity of the entire house if the OSB on a SIP starts to rot. As a result, we always made every effort to flash and waterproof each and every part of the SIP. The OSB that makes up the interior and exterior of the SIP starts to deteriorate once water sits on it for any length of time. To test this, leave a piece of OSB outside for several days. At the end of this test, the OSB will be soggy. Because the OSB provides the strength of the SIP, it is vitally important that this structural layer doesn't become compromised. Installing sky lights in SIP roof systems can be a major problem. Most skylights leak at some point during their lifecycle, and this leaking can go undetected long enough to cause major structural damage to SIP roof systems. Proper flashing and waterproofing of SIP houses concerned me so much that I hired a builder with a reputation for being the pickiest water-proofer around. I told him that he was in charge of the houses made of SIPs, and to spare no expense while ensuring those houses were flashed properly.

It is extremely important to flash window and door openings in a thorough manner so water can never enter. When remodeling, it becomes apparent that all windows leak a little water, because most areas around windows contain at least a small degree of rot. Take extra care to flash areas of the house that are prone to pooling water or large amounts of water; these areas leak water in most houses and will destroy the integrity of a SIP in a relatively short amount of time.

The biggest difference between ICFs and SIPs, besides the obvious structural differences, is connection lumber used with SIP construction. The plates, splines, and other connection lumber is not insulated, and therefore is prone to thermal pass-through. When we examine these connection points using thermal imaging cameras, the areas that allow thermal pass-through appear quite a bit colder during the winter time than the SIP itself. This difference in temperature can cause moisture. This moisture could cause some degree of decay to the OSB on the SIP if it is not monitored. The chances of this happening are slim, but still worth mentioning. Many who use

SIPs figure that the area of the wall that has thermal pass-through is minimal compared to the total conditioned area of the panel.

The cost of using SIPs for the exterior envelope of the home can be reasonable if the homeowner and/or builder understands what it takes to install SIPs. In fact, I know from experience that SIPs are the best value in exterior envelope construction of all the others technologies mentioned in this book. When combined with other building technologies, SIPs are hands down, the best value for the dollar in green building. Labor is the largest cost on any project and using SIPs means using less labor, if the team is prepared.

Using SIPs is more efficient than conventional framing, because when the wall is tipped up and secured, it is done. The SIP already has the exterior sheathing on it, is insulated, and is ready to be wired by the electrician. It is not uncommon for a medium-sized, two-story house to have all of its exterior SIP walls set in a day. This savings in time means big savings in money.

Social Media Callout Box

(Post the sentence below to your social media account.)

Labor is the largest cost on any project and using SIPs means using less labor, if the team is prepared.

When it comes to costs, an SIP home will be about five percent higher than a well-built, well-insulated conventional stick-built home—not enough to raise fair value appraisal issues for a lender. Remember that when using SIPs, there usually is less labor used to put up the same amount of SIP wall as a stick-framed wall. So even though the cost of a SIP package is higher than the cost of a lumber package, the labor is less for the SIPs, so the costs are nearly a wash. A SIP house is overwhelmingly more airtight and energy efficient than a conventional stick-framed house, and the costs are not that far apart, making the SIP an attractive option.

An SIP nightmare

Just as I warned about ICF construction, it's extremely important that you are crystal clear about how the materials will be delivered to your job site. I learned that the hard way on an all-SIP house we built once. The house was to be built on an elevated series of piers instead of a normal crawl space or basement. We were excited to apply the experience and techniques we learned from other SIP houses on this job. I spent several hours with the SIP manufacturer, and even designed the shipment so that we could unload and maneuver the SIPs in our tight work area.

I will never forget the phone call I received, which began like this: "I thought you sat down and talked to these idiots about the SIP delivery." Even though I had worked with the SIP manufacturer to design the way the SIPs would be delivered, the delivery was changed by the shipping company in order to fit more panels on the trailer. The jobsite had no extra room because it was right on a lake and the driveway was narrow with no turnaround. The load that was sent to us was stacked really high, and had the first floor SIPs on the top, meaning they would be at the bottom of the pile when unloaded and stacked on the ground. Luckily the crew on the jobsite was bright enough to do what they had to do to set the SIPs in a proper order as they unloaded the truck.

Additionally, there was a change at the last minute on the order, and we ended up receiving an SIP that was the entire length of an upstairs wall! The panel was at least twenty feet long and eight feet wide. We did not have the means to lift this panel to the upper floor, because we had no idea that we'd need to rent equipment to set the SIPs. What could we do? We ended up building a ramp to the upper subfloor, and pushing the panel up the ramp—not an easy task. Luckily we had four guys working at the site, or we would have never been able to get that SIP up onto the second floor to set it.

This may seem like a small matter, but I cannot emphasize enough that when you are working with non-traditional building methods, you need to stay on top of the way those materials are delivered to the job site. Work closely with the salesman and the shipping company to make sure you don't lose precious (and expensive) time trying to unload the materials.

Are SIPs for you?

There are a lot of advantages to building with SIPs. Although slightly more expensive, when you take into consideration that the wall is already insulated and makes drywall, siding, and trim more efficient than any other type of building, SIPs are actually quite reasonably priced. SIPs provide near-continuous insulation and can contribute to extreme air tightness. SIPs reduce labor costs associated

Social Media Callout Box
(Post the sentence below to your social media account.)

A house made of SIPs is nearly soundproof, and creates a very comfortable, warm, and quiet home.

with building a home by reducing the amount of time it takes to install the outside walls and insulation. A house made of SIPs is nearly soundproof, and creates a very comfortable, warm, and quiet home. SIPs also help reduce waste and scrap associated with conventional building by providing precut, computer-design panels.

The major disadvantage of SIPs is that the outer sides are made of wood. This makes proper water proofing measures essential to their longevity. The outer layer of SIPs is made of Oriented Strand Board (OSB), which deteriorates quickly when exposed to moisture. This OSB is the structural support of the SIP panels. If the OSB rots out, then the integrity of the home is compromised. Another disadvantage of SIPs is staging them on a jobsite. SIPs arrive on a semi trailer (usually), and they are loaded based on logistics, not order of installation. This causes confusion, congestion, and hassles for those who are off-loading the SIP delivery truck. Sub-contractors have a hard time with SIPs because they are not used to working with them. However, sub-contractors who have experience with SIPs find they are actually more efficient to work with, since everything is made in the factory, including all the electrical wire runs.

When it comes to value and benefits, SIPs are the most economical choice for a building envelope. Anyone with building experience can install SIPs, and SIPs can save the installer a large amount of time. With proper attention paid to flashing and waterproofing, a house with SIPs can stand for many generations. SIPs can be installed by any builder with proper training. In most cases, homeowners who were considering framing a home decide to switch to SIP construction once they see that the cost is very close (within a percent or two) to conventional building. Trusses can be used with SIPs, and are the preferred roofing system over SIP roof systems due to ease of installation. Normally, trusses are ordered with ener-gy heels, and spray foam is used to compliment the tightness of the SIPs. SIPs are the perfect fit for a project on a budget that demands energy efficiency and minimal air infiltration.

But why not have the best of two worlds? After we built a few SIP houses, we learned the best way to incorporate SIPs into our building systems was to use ICFs for the basement and SIPs for all exterior walls, and roof trusses with energy heels in the attic. For insulation, we found that using spray foam insulation, preferably agricultural-based product, on the rim board of the floor systems and in the attic gave us the best results on our energy tests.

When I finally get around to building my own house, that's exactly what I will do—use ICFs for the basement and SIP for the rest.

7 ADVANCED FRAMING

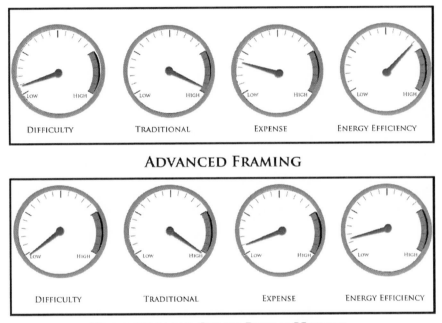

ADVANCED FRAMING

TRADITIONAL STICK BUILT HOUSE

I used to get into arguments with other builders about how inefficient stick-built houses could be. I distinctly recall a conversation with a builder at a home show who said people were "stupid" to build with ICFs, since he could achieve the same results by stick framing a home. Naturally, as Mr. ICF, I took offense to what he said, and gave him an earful of what I thought about him and his stick building. I didn't believe that a stick-built house could be very energy efficient—that is, until a job came along that had to be stick-built to fall within the homeowner's budget. I actually became excited, because I had heard of advanced framing—a special technique for constructing a stick-built home—and was eager to give it a try. Once we built an advanced frame house and I saw how efficient it ended up being, I became a believer.

Advanced framing is a progressive style of framing a house's building envelope. Advanced framing is used to reduce the amount of framing lumber, and reduce thermal bridging through the wall studs. Normally, advanced framing calls for 2x6 wood studs that are spaced at twenty-four inches on center. The spacing of the studs is intended to line up with roof trusses in order to transfer the load of the truss to the footing, and also to eliminate unneeded lumber. Advanced framing is more widely used currently than ICFs or SIPs because the process is not much different than conventional framing, and framers grasp the concept of advanced framing quicker than the other forms of building mentioned in this book. Panelized or pre-fabricated walls also fit under the category of advanced framing. Several builders have walls pre-made in shops that are then transported to the jobsite and installed. Panelized systems can be an efficient way of building and, when mastered, can be a notably economical way of building.

The corners used in advanced framing are built with two studs that form what the industry calls an "L corner". This "L" allows the corner to be insulated in an area that normally is not. The advantages of insulating a corner are abundant. During the cold months of the year, corners of rooms that are poorly insulated have been known to grow mold as a result of the temperature differential created by thermal pass-through. Moisture forms whenever two different temperatures meet in a location. If the temperature difference is great in a location, such as an un-insulated corner, then the level of moisture is very high and creates a favorable area for mold growth. Mold is hazardous to your health, and more and more people are appearing at doctors' offices infested with mold from their homes.

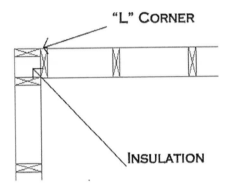

"L" CORNER

INSULATION

The same phenomenon can occur in any area of a wall that is not insulated. Many times, mold grows at the top of a wall and along a ceiling, because there is no insulation present in this area. The cold outside air can pass directly through these un-insulated areas at an alarming rate, which almost immediately causes moisture. On thermal images of these areas, it is not uncommon to see an interior temperature in the seventies and a spot on the wall in the forties. This is a problem! You can expect this same phenomenon at sill plates, headers, and any other point in the wall that is un-insulated.

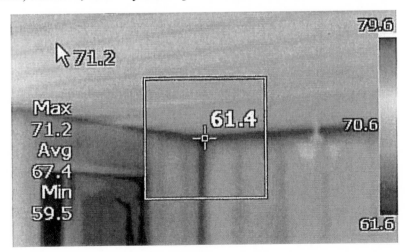

Thermal pass-through with advanced framing

The goal of advanced framing is to reduce the number of framing members to not only save material and trees, but also to help reduce thermal bridging (thermal pass-through). For an advanced frame wall to achieve similar levels of reduced air infiltration and increased insulation value (among other things) as an ICF or SIP, thermal pass-through measures must be implemented.

For a 2X4 studded wall, siding, sheathing, wall studs, and interior wall covering add up to about an R-6 insulating value. At every spot where a stud attaches to an exterior wall, the insulating value goes from about R-19 (with fiberglass batt insulation in wall cavities) to an R-value of about 6. In this scenario, if the wall studs were pushed all together, then a fair portion of the house is left un-insulated. Advanced framing addresses thermal pass-through by using 2x6 studs spaced further apart than usual. This reduces the number of studs through which cold or warm air can pass, and increases the amount of insulation that a wall can have.

To slow thermal pass-through and prevent air infiltration on an advanced frame wall, a layer of foam board should be applied over the exterior sheathing of the wall and taped at each seam. Most homes with a quarter-inch Dow board installed in this manner notice less thermal pass-through. One-inch foam board is optimal to slow thermal pass-through; any thicker foam inhibits siding fasteners from sticking properly to the exterior sheathing below the foam board. Most builders who use advanced framing use open cell spray foam to insulate between the 2x6 studs. This makes the wall very airtight, and the open cell spray foam expands and contracts with the movement of the wood in the wall over the seasons.

Sill seal is a sheet of foam used between the foundation wall and the sill plate sits on the foundation wall. Most times, this sill seal is installed and never again considered. This is a problematic area on all stick-built houses, and an area prone to moisture build up and possibly rotting wood and mold. Sill seal is not the only answer for sealing this area of a house because the sill plate is never completely tight over the entire run of the foundation wall (due to the distance between anchor bolts and the unevenness of the top of the foundation wall).

Most states require the use of anchor bolts or straps that secure the sill plate to within a foot of a corner and four feet on center along the rest of the wall. This causes the board to warp and only become tight every four feet or wherever there is an anchor bolt or strap. Air leaks through the gaps between the sill plate and the top of the foundation wall. The same thing occurs on the top of an ICF wall where the top plate is. If the top plate is set on top of the foam of the ICF, there will be major air leakage there. It is important to set the top plate of the ICF into the foam so there is not a gap.

An advanced frame house that is well insulated and geared towards slowing thermal pass-through behaves differently than a conventionally framed house. Once a house becomes tight and well insulated, even the smallest air leak becomes a problem. These air leaks around the house create almost a vacuum, and air can rush

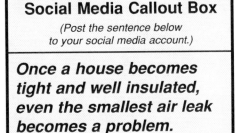

Social Media Callout Box

(Post the sentence below to your social media account.)

Once a house becomes tight and well insulated, even the smallest air leak becomes a problem.

through these areas. The gaps along the sill plate and foundation wall are the biggest air leaking gaps that a house can have. During the cold months, cold air can rush through these cracks so quickly, that the anchor bolts and nails in the framing will actually collect frost. This frost doesn't just occur in one spot; it spreads to all the other metal near the air leak. This frost turns to moisture when the air warms up, and the wood absorbs the moisture. Wood will begin to mold and rot if this situation goes on over the seasons.

The only way to prevent this air leakage from occurring is to caulk the area before it is covered with the interior wall covering. If there is no wall covering, then carefully applying the caulk so it looks nice is a good idea. Traditional builders will say that the weight of the house will settle the sill plate down and close these air gaps; in my experience, this is not true. Energy auditors continue to see the sill plate areas of the home leak for decades.

If an advanced frame house sits on an ICF foundation, which is the preferred method, remember to set the sill plate down into the ICF, so there is foam on the outside of the sill plate. This will eliminate any air leaks in this area. To set the sill plate into the ICF, the installers must make sure that the concrete poured in the form is at least an inch and a half lower than the top of the form. This way the anchor bolts can be set to code and the sill plate can be bolted down with no sill seal.

Keeping it tight

All houses that have a framed floor system on top of a foundation have an area that must be insulated. This area is located between each floor joist and along the rim joist of the floor system.

Insulating this area is crucial to prevent cold spots in the floor and resultant moisture issues. To insulate these areas, I have found that open cell spray foam is the best choice. Using spray foam in these areas is a great compliment to the other insulated areas of an energy-efficient home.

To get as tight a house as possible with framing of any kind, including advanced framing, you should caulk every crack, crevice, and spot where woods connect to each other. Stopping even the faintest of air leaks will create an even more energy efficient home. With ICFs and earth shelter construction, this is normally not necessary because the wall system is inherently airtight.

Advanced framing is the closet to traditional building, so you won't have to deal with some of the problems unique to less-conventional methods of construction mentioned in this book. Deliveries are no different from conventional frame deliveries, and don't require any extra equipment. Sub-contractors require no additional training, as they might when using SIPs or ICFs. And scheduling the building process on an advanced frame house is exactly the same as scheduling a conventional home.

The cost of advanced framing can be comparable to conventional framing, unless you take measures to stop thermal bridging on the houses (something I highly recommend). The additional costs of exterior foam board, spray foam insulation, caulking, and everything else that goes into the construction of an energy efficient advanced frame home can approach the cost of using SIPs for the exterior shell.

Practical considerations

Because the spacing of the wall studs in an advanced-frame house is at twenty four inches on center, 5/8" drywall is used on the walls, not the standard 1/2" drywall. I remember getting a call from one of the trim guys who told me that all of our preordered jamb extensions for the windows in the house were short of the drywall. This required adding a 1/8" piece of extension material to the jamb so that the window casing could be put on properly. After that day, we started to order our windows for advanced frame houses with no jamb extensions, and then crafting our own jamb extensions on site. This lends the finish work around the window a more uniformed appearance.

Hanging cabinets on an advanced frame wall can be challenging due to the wider spacing of the wall studs. Planning in advance can assure that the cabinets can be hung properly and will be strong enough to support a cupboard full of dishes. Some builders will inset a 2x6 sideways into the studs of the wall and wherever the upper cabinets will hang. If we have a kitchen layout, we hang plywood on the wall to hang cabinets, just like we would do in an ICF home.

Is an advanced-frame house efficient when it comes to energy conservation? I'll answer with a story about a fully advanced frame house we built in southern Michigan. It was set up to use passive solar energy—built in a field with a great southern exposure for the living areas of the house. We built the house out of 2x6 wall studs and put 1/4" foam insulation over the outside sheathing. The house had vinyl siding over the foam board, and when it came to the insulation in the walls and attic, I budgeted in spray foam insulation. Not only did we insulate the wall cavities with spray foam, but also the rim joist areas of the home, and we sprayed the foam directly to the bottom of the roof deck in the attic.

This house utilized a propane-fired, forced-air heating system that the homeowners installed themselves to save money. On the main floor of the house, the homeowners had a wood burning cook stove, which they also wanted to use to help heat the home. Initially, the wood stove was missing an important part, so the homeowners were unable to use the woodstove as winter approached. Then one day, the homeowner called me and asked me to stop by to inspect their propane furnace to determine why it wasn't working.

Before I drove out to their house to see what the problem was, I asked them a few questions to see if we might figure it out over the phone. I learned that for three nights in a row the temperature outside fell below freezing, yet the house was reasonably warm despite the fact that neither the furnace nor the wood stove were working.

"Do you mean to tell me that you had no heat whatsoever during those below-freezing nights, and your house was still warm?" I asked.

"Yes, isn't that amazing?" she answered proudly.

The advanced frame house was so airtight and well insulated that the homeowner never knew the heating system was not working. The sun warmed the house during the day and then held enough heat to keep the homeowners warm until the sun came out the next day. The house went three days and nights without heat while nighttime temperatures fell to twenty-eight degrees Fahrenheit. The temperature in the house stayed in the upper sixties each sunny day, and fell into the lower sixties on the cloudy day. Pretty remarkable for a stick-built house!

> **Social Media Callout Box**
> *(Post the sentence below to your social media account.)*
>
> ***The advanced frame house was so airtight that the homeowner never knew the heating system was not working.***

This advanced frame house was built for the same cost, if not a little less, as comparable stick-built houses; we just shuffled the budget around and put more money into the insulation of the home. The homeowners and I got creative with flooring and kitchen options, and came up with the extra money needed to cover the cost of the spray foam insulation. I am still amazed how that house and the other advanced frame homes that we have built have performed.

Stories like these aren't uncommon, but heard all over the country. In the past, this kind of performance was only achieved with ICFs and SIPs. The idea that someone can create a stick-built house to capture and contain heat or cool air is a new idea for most builders. Nevertheless, with a focus on using the best forms of insulation, sealing all problematic spots, and considering thermal protection, builders have been able to achieve incredible efficiency with stick-built houses. The building industry got a much needed intelligence when builders were forced to start their own building businesses after persistent layoffs. Engineers who started building businesses have created highly energy-efficient homes using nearly the same amount of material as conventional builders.

Understanding that stick-built houses can and will achieve the highest levels of energy efficiency has helped to reshape the building industry, as advanced framing doesn't stray too far from tradition. Energy codes in most states require builders to insulate basement walls now, which complements the extra efforts these builders are putting into crafting airtight homes. For many years, builders fought against energy codes, fearing the cost of required upgrades would negatively affect the building market. This simply has not been the case; people will pay extra costs if they understand the benefits they will get for their investment. The economy has slowed the building industry, not state and national energy codes.

An advanced frame house that has been built with all of the materials needed to make it extremely airtight can cost up to ten percent more than a conventional build. At that point, I believe using SIPs for the exterior envelope of the home is a better value than advanced framing a home. SIPs remain the best value in building; to understand why, visit the chapter on SIPs in this book.

Growing popularity of advanced framing

If advanced framing technology has existed for some time, why isn't it more popular? The answer is rooted in communication: we just didn't hear about it until the internet allowed people to communicate what they were up to. Builders around the country have utilized advanced framing for many years, and have become better and more efficient as technology has permitted. Traditionally, builders didn't know (or worse, didn't care) how a house performed because fuel prices were low, and even the worst insulated homes didn't take a ton of money to heat or cool. Most builders installed an unnecessarily large heating systems, just so there was enough power to make up for drafty houses. Traditional builders will say that you don't want to build a house too tight because it will be unsafe. There is some truth in that, so be sure to learn about proper air exchange later in this book.

Like other areas of this green movement, things reached a head all at once, because more people became concerned with the state of the country. Rising fuel prices get attention. A traditionally built house uses an incredible amount of fuel to heat and cool, and consequently people have looked to get out of those homes and into something more energy efficient. In fact, during the housing boom of the 90s, less than one percent of the homes built could be considered energy efficient.

One of the biggest reasons the industry has seen a shift toward green building is that engineers who lost their jobs in their respective industries started building companies of their own. As a result, the building industry gained an incredible "think tank." I know a few builders who lost their jobs as engineers and then started building companies, and they've built incredibly energy efficient homes without detouring too far from traditional methods.

The work of these engineers in the building industry helped to increase the energy efficiency of stick-built houses. The engineers and others who started building companies were not traditional builders and their ability to think outside of the normal building box was better than most builders. As a result, this new generation of builders started blower door testing stick-built houses, and working to improve the performance of stick built-houses. Because of the connections that these people had, more and more pressure was put on the state governments to implement a model energy code so that all houses would be built to use less energy. This caused quite a stir in the building industry, a stir that I feel was important for creating much needed change in how houses were being built.

Advanced framing seemed like a 'no brainer' to this new generation of builders just as the demand started to grow for more energy efficient homes. This new group of non-traditional builders started their companies as a shift in generations occurred. This new group of buyers was demanding a certain performance out of the houses they wanted to build or buy and could not find builders to build the kinds of houses that they wanted. This new generation of builder gladly built homes for this group of buyers and saw success doing it in uncertain economic times.

Should you use advanced framing for your next house?

A major advantage of advanced framing is its similarity to conventional framing, making this form of construction more inviting to traditional builders. Extremely airtight homes have been achieved using advanced framing, and energy audits compare very closely to homes built with ICFs and SIPs. Advanced framing is no different for sub-contractors. Pass-through(s) to the exterior of the house are addressed by the insulators, and require no additional work for the sub-contractors, as with ICFs and SIPs.

Advanced framing is the least confusing style of building for suppliers, workers, and homeowners, and this is an advantage; fewer issues arise during this type of construction. Materials can be supplied as they normally would, with the same trucks, and this is one consideration that keeps advanced framing the most favorable form of building of the four mentioned in this book.

Advanced framing requires no special equipment beyond what a traditional builder would possess. This is an incredible advantage, because builders can adjust to the demand of the market without investing any money in tools. The major investment is in time and learning the aspects of advanced framing.

A major disadvantage of advanced framing is the extra material and effort it takes to make the walls airtight and well insulated. By the time you add up the cost of exterior foam board, the labor to install the foam, and everything associated with making the wall meet high efficiency standards, you have reached the price of using SIPs. Pricing of an advanced frame house can take practice before a builder knows how to adjust for the added materials and labor.

Another disadvantage is that you must use 5/8-inch drywall on studs that are spaced on 24-inch centers to keep the drywall from bowing over time. This thicker drywall then creates a problem with jamb extensions for windows. Windows must be ordered without jamb extensions, and onsite jamb extensions must be made to accommodate the 1/8-inch to1/4-inch thicker walls. If a builder does not plan for this, then money is lost for the extra time it takes to correct the problem.

A minor disadvantage of advanced framing is the lack of studs on which to mount cabinets or hang pictures. This can be a problem with custom cabinets, or with homeowners who like to hang decoration on their walls. Like other issues, these minor disadvantages can be addressed and handled proactively to avoid major issues in the future.

Social Media Callout Box
(Post the sentence below to your social media account.)

Advanced framing is a great way for someone on a budget to get a tight, energy efficient home.

Advanced framing is a great way for someone on a budget to get a tight, energy efficient home, but it will take some effort to achieve this. Those who live in advanced framed houses (and pay lower energy bills) quickly realize that the extra effort is worth it.

8 EARTH SHELTERS

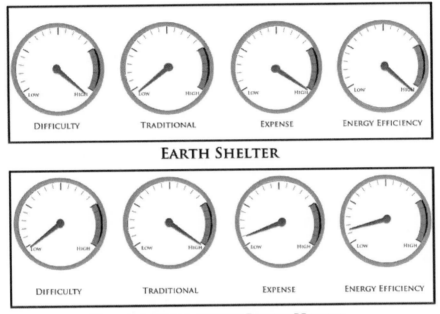

DIFFICULTY   TRADITIONAL   EXPENSE   ENERGY EFFICIENCY

EARTH SHELTER

DIFFICULTY   TRADITIONAL   EXPENSE   ENERGY EFFICIENCY

TRADITIONAL STICK BUILT HOUSE

I remember when I first got the call to build an earth shelter house. Until then, my familiarity with earth shelters was admittedly thin, so I had to do what many people do: research on the internet. What I found were a multitude of earth shelter design styles. The project that I signed on to help build was a dome style earth shelter, which is supposedly the strongest form of earth shelter due to the arch-like design. I had to give the project a lot of thought because I had no idea how we were going to build it.

An earth shelter house is pretty self-explanatory—it's a structure that is partially or completely covered in earth. Earth sheltering is not new; in fact, earth sheltering is one of the oldest forms of housing. For thousands of years, people have used the earth to insulate their homes, escape the elements, and ensure safety.

> ### Social Media Callout Box
> *(Post the sentence below to your social media account.)*
>
> **For thousands of years, people have used the earth to insulate their homes, escape the elements, and ensure safety.**

When the settlers moved west to claim their Homestead Act land in the middle to late 1800s, they were faced with a harsh reality: there were no trees in the grass lands of the central and western states. No trees meant that the settlers had to rely on earth sheltering to build houses. They survived in this manner until train tracks were laid, enabling shipment of much-needed building supplies.

Earth sheltering has come a long way since the 1800s. There are many forms available today, each with their own characteristics and benefits. Dome style earth shelters have grown in popularity over the past decade because they provide the greatest strength. Large domes create more space on exposed walls for windows. When combined with a passive solar design, any style earth shelter house can heat naturally in the cold months by using only the sun.

Earth sheltering, from a performance standpoint, makes a lot of sense. The science behind building into earth, which maintains constant temperature, is undeniable. For many people, a major motivation for building with this technology is that earth shelter structures are extremely energy efficient.

Energy efficiency and earth shelters

In an above ground house in the Midwest, exterior walls that are exposed to the open air can be subjected to a wide range of temperatures. Even the best forms of construction that offer superior insulation properties and air tightness can be strained by the range of -10 degrees Fahrenheit to 100 degrees Fahrenheit. This unusually wide range of temperatures can be difficult to prepare for, and can result in high energy bills. The Midwest is not like other areas of the country where the temperature swing is not as great.

Energy performance problems in climates with wide ranging temperatures can be explained with math and science. If the range of temperature and weather conditions is considered the independent variable in an equation, it is immediately apparent that the house is going to have an incredible force put upon it. If you recall from math class, an independent variable (changing temperatures and conditions outside a house) is a variable that can freely take on different values. Simple algebra helps explain how a home owner or builder can determine which form of construction will be the most efficient.

To remove the guess work from this equation, keep in mind that the less a variable changes, the easier it is to solve an equation. It's hard to determine which exterior envelope is the best option when temperature and conditions constantly change.

When an earth shelter is covered on most of the structure, an incredible phenomenon occurs. The variable in the equation becomes a constant, and determining how the home will perform becomes simple. An earth shelter that is completely covered with at least two feet of earth will never drop below ground temperature, because

Social Media Callout Box

(Post the sentence below to your social media account.)

An earth shelter that is covered with at least two feet of earth will never drop below ground temperature.

ground temperature doesn't change in a statistically significant manner that deep in the ground. It follows, then, that the heating of the home becomes more efficient, and requires less costly solutions.

If you are tracking with me so far, then we have to examine another question. Most earth shelters have an exposed wall or two. How does this exposed wall affect the efficiency of the home? If you consider the effect of a breach in a system, the exposed exterior wall on an earth shelter can make or break the structure. Depending on where the home is located in the country, the exterior wall can be built out of varying materials and still achieve great performance. In an area where the variable temperature range is greater, there is only one choice, in my experience, for the exterior exposed wall of an earth shelter: ICF.

If you take into consideration the motivations behind a person's desire to build an earth shelter, you will notice that the ICF is a perfect fit for the exposed exterior wall. Safety is an underlying concern for this market segment, and the reinforced concrete that sits inside of the ICF wall is nearly impenetrable. Using ICF on the exposed exterior wall of an earth shelter structure will deliver an extremely tough wall between the inside of the home and the elements outside, and the ICF wall will also be nearly as efficient as the earth shelter structure itself. I have learned that ICFs and earth shelter structures are a perfect complement to each other.

It is proven that an earth shelter will never drop below ground temperature as long as the structure remains sealed to the outside elements. This means that the inside of the structure will never drop below the mid to upper fifty degree range. Those who join the earth shelter club quickly learn that membership has its privileges. These privileges include never worrying about frozen water pipes or heating system malfunctions.

Challenges with earth shelters

Earth shelters are amazing places to live in, but they are not issue-free. There are several concerns and details that are paramount when considering an earth shelter build. The majority of earth shelter systems sold in this country are sold directly to homeowners, which I've learned (as both builder and consultant) can cause many problems. Homeowners will often purchase an earth shelter system prior to identifying a builder. As a result, code officials and building inspectors can become unsure of the project and create road blocks to progress. This is not a bad thing; a building inspector's job is to protect the homeowner either from a builder or from the homeowner's own work. In states where homeowners can draw their own permits to build their homes themselves, building inspectors will pay close attention to homeowner-run projects.

Before building an earth shelter, hire a soil engineer to check out the building site, prior to any excavation and prior to sending any prints to a structural engineer. The soil engineer will determine the types of soil present and the resultant weight capacity and pressure. The structural engineer must know the soil composition on and around the earth shelter structure to determine how strong the structure needs to be to withstand the pressure of those soils. This can be an expensive procedure, but it is a required and necessary cost. Never break ground without knowing what kind of soils you are dealing with.

Varying styles of earth shelters are better suited to some areas than others, due to varying soil types. Those who want to build a concrete structure underground with a flat or slightly sloping, earth-covered roof will find it difficult to get design approval from building officials. This is especially true in areas with significant clay deposits. Clay becomes extremely heavy when it collects water, and it also traps water against the earth shelter structure, which can cause leaking. The best advice that any professional could give: make sure that any earth shelter structure has been reviewed and stamped by an engineer who is licensed to practice in the state where the structure is to be built; and have engineer-stamped building plans in hand before you ever talk to a building official. The reason is, building officials will require engineer-affirmed plans to proceed, and having an engineered stamped set of plans and soil reports ahead of time builds confidence in the building official. There is nothing a building official can say about the strength of the structure if an engineer stamped the drawings.

There are areas of the country where earth shelters are more popular. In these areas, finding qualified water proofers and insulators is not that hard. In areas where there are few earth shelters, finding a subcontractor who is comfortable guaranteeing their work and doing a good job will be difficult. There are no manufacturers that I can recommend that will feel comfortable offering any sort of long-lasting warranty if their waterproofing product is used underground. Also, there are too many variables to guarantee that an earth shelter won't leak. Despite considerable waterproofing, there are earth shelter structures around the United States that still leak. In the building industry there is a saying: all earth shelters leak. There is truth to that statement, and a lot of the leaking occurs when the earth shelters are built in soils with clay and other non-pervious materials.

Building and consulting on earth shelters taught me a lot about waterproofing. The very first earth shelter project we built had five underground domes. The homeowner hired a waterproofer that, unbeknownst to us, thinned the waterproofing material with mineral spirits for easier application. As a result, instead of a continuous 60mil thickness of rubber membrane (what the manufacturer recommended), the majority of the surface area they waterproofed had only a thickness of 6mil. To understand how bad this is, 6mil is approximately as thick as a piece of copy paper. Each of the domes leaked with every rain, and we had to build water diverting systems for all domes to prevent water from reaching this thin waterproofing. Going with the lowest bidder is not always the best idea. Despite repeated calls, the waterproofer never took care of the waterproofing issues on that project.

The builder and the homeowner

I vividly recall a specific earth shelter project that is a great example of why it is important for homeowners to find the right builder to help them with their project. A homeowner in Michigan ordered a dome style kit from a company in Colorado. The homeowner had worked with the company for more than six months to get the design of the earth shelter down to something she wanted. The goal of the homeowner, who was in the process of finding a suitable builder, was to begin her project in the late summer and have the majority of the outside structure installed and water tight before the winter. A water tight structure would permit interior work during the winter months, and then the structure could be backfilled in the late spring.

The schedule for the project looked great on paper, and the homeowner took steps to get the project started before she selected me as the builder. I went out to the building site, looked it over, and suggested a soil test by an engineer, which occurred before the site was excavated. She knew that the soil was mostly clay at the build site and was willing to assume any risk that backfilling with clay in Michigan would present. I wanted to make sure from the beginning that she knew that working in clay could be time consuming, expensive, and may not work with an earth shelter. The next step was to try to assign a cost to the project, so the homeowner and I started to interview potential sub-contractors.

We soon realized that not everyone was excited about building the project as we were. I had seen this before with other projects, and learned to just keep interviewing companies until one came along who was excited about a challenge, like an earth shelter. Excavators were leery of working in the clay and offered every reason why that was a bad idea—including that clay would destroy the structure as it filled with water and settled. A few excavators told the homeowner and me that we were crazy for even thinking of building the project. I knew how to diffuse nay-sayers from past projects, so I was able to turn the conversation from being negative to positive. This is one of the key reasons for sourcing an experienced building team for non-traditional building projects.

Once the homeowner and I selected an excavator, it was time to search out a concrete company that could build the elaborate earthquake resistant footings that engineers from Utah had designed for the footing system. The earth shelter had an open-end and a closed-end dome, which meant there were radii on the back side of the domes. Inset every six inches into each footing on the radii were insert sleeves for rebar. The building prints were clear as to where the placement of the rebar sleeves were located, and also provided clear dimensions for the radius work. The design was located out west, so the incredibly large footings and flatwork (which would be the finished floor) had to be a mono-pour, where all of the concrete was poured at the same time, footings first, then the floor finished.

Concrete companies that did commercial work would find this type of construction difficult but not impossible. The homeowner and I began to interview concrete companies, and once again found out that concrete companies were not as excited about the project as we were. After searching for a few weeks, the homeowner found a concrete company that was willing to do the work, but for an extra charge due to the challenging design.

The homeowner contacted the earth shelter company to place her order once she had a better idea of what the project was going to cost. From the beginning, I insisted that she was low on her budget, and agreed to work with her to get as much as possible done on the project for as little money as possible. The earth shelter company assured the kit would be delivered on time, so the homeowner ordered the kit.

We agreed on September first as a start date, and a deposit secured the plan. In order to explore similar projects and the homeowner's needs, we flew together to Washington State to view an earth shelter under construction. What we learned from the visit and the on-site builder eventually saved the homeowner tens of thousands of dollars, far more than the trip cost. I recommend visiting projects that are similar to your designs before a build.

After our trip out west, the homeowner got the excavator started on the site and he worked for a week straight to clear a large hill. Once the space for the shelter was dug out, I visited the site to set corner stakes to ensure the excavation dimensions were correct for a clean fit. Assuming that a structure will fit anywhere is not a good idea—a builder should always verify first. With the project site excavated and the perimeter of the project staked, it was time to get the concrete work started.

During this time, I was working two and a half hours away from the project site, attempting to wrap up another job. The concrete company wanted me to stake the south facing walls of the earth shelter since it was crucial that this project utilized passive solar.

The south facing wall was over one hundred feet long, and the concrete company didn't want the liability of laying that important area out. This was not communicated to the homeowner until the concrete company's crew was on site and ready to work. Luckily, I was able to pull off the other job and race two and a half hours north to work with the concrete company. I had grown to expect last minute things when working so closely with homeowners, but then again, the building industry can be a world of racing around and managing communication.

The homeowner called the earth shelter company to confirm the earth shelter kit would be delivered on schedule, and was forced to leave a message because no one answered. The concrete work had already been initiated because the earth shelter company took the homeowner's money and guaranteed a delivery date. After a week of waiting for a return call, the homeowner once again called the earth shelter company. When they answered, they actually asked her who she was! She asked to confirm the order and the agreed upon ship date, and was told that nothing was on order because they were waiting for their engineer in Utah to finish the building prints. My heart sank when I learned that we wouldn't be starting on September first as we had agreed. As a builder, I was stuck because I had no other work lined up for my employees.

While the news was fresh on the homeowner's mind, the concrete company was working long hours to get the concrete work done on time. The completion date for the concrete coincided with the original delivery date of the earth shelter kit, which was apparently not going to arrive as scheduled. The tight timeline was crucial; the earth shelter needed to be built and waterproofed by the end of December so it would be weather tight for the winter. None of us knew what to say.

We ultimately decided to move forward as if we were going to receive the kit on time. The homeowner began interviewing plumbers to work on pipes beneath the concrete. She had a hard time finding a plumber to give her a quote due to the project's scope. Then she went through two plumbers during the concrete phase because the plumbers were unable to comprehend how the different domes would connect together. The plumbing was no different than in any other houses, save a little math to work out the radii portions. As it stood, half of the rough-in plumbing they installed was incorrectly located, which would later alter the design that the homeowner had waited so long to get drawn up. I had signed on as a consultant and builder, and this was a homeowner contracted project, which meant she had the final say on material and sub-contractor selection.

The concrete work took over a month to complete, and the start date of September first was rapidly approaching. After several unreturned phone calls to the kit company, the homeowner finally learned that a delivery on or around the target date was still a possibility. I was excited to get started, and thought, "Wow, we just dodged a huge bullet!"

The concrete company finished their work after September first, just in time for the homeowner to find out that her earth shelter order had not been shipped. According to the seller, the kit was made in California, and then shipped to Arizona before being shipped to the jobsite. After several calls to California, the earth shelter company found out that the kit was never made because an engineering question (for the engineer in Utah!) went unanswered. With October rapidly approaching and winter around the corner, the homeowner and I were beginning to get worried. I couldn't give my employees a solid answer as to whether or not they would have work. It was a difficult time for my company, because the future of it hinged on an unknown engineer in Utah.

As Thanksgiving neared the homeowner grew irate. The possibility of getting the earth shelter weather proofed in time for winter was fading. I had been taking steps to line up another project when I received a phone call from the homeowner stating the earth shelter kit would be delivered just before Thanksgiving.

Finally, on the Wednesday before Thanksgiving, well after dark, the homeowner and her family unloaded a semi of mismarked steel, and laid it out in the field in front of the project. The trucker showed up unannounced to the jobsite, late in the evening. All of the steel was unloaded on a road with deep ditches to either side, blocking traffic for several hours.

Our new goal now was to work around the clock to erect the structures and get them weather proofed by the end of December. It just so happened to be the largest residential earth shelter project ever built with five underground domes, so our goal proved a tad lofty. Ultimately, the crews worked in the bitterly cold winter weather to build the structures, framed inside the structures, and prepared the domes to be weather proofed in the spring. Working in the winter slowed the progress, as daily routines included removing snow, pulling stuck delivery trucks, and scraping ice off of all the steel. The crews worked around the clock and labor cost soared past the budgeted amount.

This story goes on and on and, in fact, we filmed the entire ordeal. The videos are online at my website: www.adambearup.com if you are interested in viewing them. From excavating, to concrete, and sub-par water proofing, this project saw every possible problem. The homeowner and I worked together to finish the project, which still leaks. When people hear this story, they immediately ask if, had I known then what I know now, would I still take the project. Without hesitation, my response is always an excited, "You bet I would! Those were the two best years of my life!" Sometimes we learn the most from our biggest problems, and this proved to be the equivalent of earning a Ph.D. in earth structures.

> **Social Media Callout Box**
> *(Post the sentence below to your social media account.)*
>
> ***Sometimes we learn the most from our biggest problems.***

Why build an earth shelter?

Like any structure, an earth shelter presents its own set of challenges. Earth shelter structures need to be properly ventilated to prevent high humidity inside the home. Once an area of an extremely air tight house takes on moisture, it will hold that moisture unless the home breathes properly. A new term has arisen to describe the result of persistent trapped moisture: sick houses. In other words, houses that precipitate illness due to black mold and poor air quality. If a house is extremely airtight, proper air exchange measures are paramount. This is a budget item that should not be limited; every penny should be spent to make sure the house you are building exchanges air at a safe rate. An energy audit on a finished home will help you to determine what the proper air exchange is for the home. Without it, you risk the chance of becoming sick in your house.

One of the greatest advantages of an earth shelter home is the constant temperature the house maintains, thanks to the stability of ground temperature. Unlike traditional houses that must do battle with extreme internal and external temperature differences, earth shelters do not, so heating and cooling costs are extremely low.

Another advantage of the earth shelter structure is safety. With an ICF front wall on the exposed side, an earth shelter structure can

Social Media Callout Box
(Post the sentence below to your social media account.)

An earth shelter structure can withstand winds of 300 mph.

withstand winds of 300 mph, and is not as susceptible to extreme weather conditions as an above-ground home. Indeed, safety is the motivation of many people who build earth shelter houses as their primary residence. An earth shelter structure offers the ultimate in home security and is a quiet, comfortable, and a safe place to live.

Because the earth shelter project is underground, it is important that the structure is water proofed properly. There are areas on an earth shelter project that could be prone to leaks, such as the junction of concreted domes and front ICF walls. It is very difficult to waterproof these areas. Another area of concern for water infiltration is where the concrete domes meet the footings. Extra drain tile and pea gravel should be used in these areas.

Indoor air quality is a major concern in all structures that are extremely air tight, but even more so in an earth shelter project since there are no windows for ventilation. Air exchangers must be used to properly exchange all air and keep the house mold free and smelling fresh.

Earth shelter houses can pose a problem for sub-contractors. There are parts of the earth shelter that are quite different from what most builders and sub-contractors would expect. Additionally, the progressive style of building employed can make building inspectors nervous and often times this nervousness can stop a project.

Of all styles of building, earth shelter's unique construction process require the most proactivity. Earth shelter projects are notorious for going over budget, mostly due to unforeseen labor costs. The best advice one can give to avoid these labor overages? Wait to set a start date until the earth shelter kit or material is on site.

I don't want these challenges to prevent you from considering an earth shelter. They can be amazing homes, comfortable, safe, and most important, extremely energy efficient. If you work with a builder who has had experience with earth shelters, you will avoid many of the problems associated with the process of building an earth shelter.

9 PUTTING IT ALL TOGETHER

By this point, you have learned about the experiences that my team and I have had with advanced technologies. If you take anything out of the last four chapters, understand that building with these technologies for the first time can be challenging on many levels. Now, since the management style was the same on all the types of homes that we built, we can compare the efficiencies of each technology in terms of budget impact, along with energy impact. Reviewing the meters below, you can see how the four building technologies I covered compare to each other.

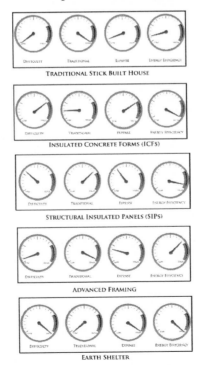

TRADITIONAL STICK BUILT HOUSE

INSULATED CONCRETE FORMS (ICFS)

STRUCTURAL INSULATED PANELS (SIPS)

ADVANCED FRAMING

EARTH SHELTER

As you can see, each of these building technologies offers attractive benefits, along with some challenges. So the question is "Can these different technologies be combined together effectively and efficiently?" In other words what about a "hybrid home?"

In the plant and animal world, hybridization occurs when the core strengths of two sub-species are combined to realize better results than each would achieve separately. Such is the case with building eco-friendly homes. Combine technologies to achieve something better than each individual technology. But the key is to combine all the elements properly. Without the correct combination of materials, processes, and technologies, a house will not become the best that it can become with regards to energy efficiency and earth friendliness. For example, if an airtight home with a superior exterior envelope is built without an air exchanger, pervasive moisture issues will result. Likewise, builders who don't understand the dynamics of home hybridization won't be able to solve problems that arise from a poor (or incomplete) mix of technologies.

We don't have to look too far past Newton's third law of motion to understand why everything that makes up a house either works with or against the other components of a house. Newton's third law can be roughly truncated to mean all actions induce reactions—forces are interdependent. With this in mind, you can see why a house needs to have the correct combination of materials, processes and technologies.

I found this out the hard way while building a home early in my career. The house was designed to host a wine cellar beneath the front porch, which we built out of ICFs, like the rest of the exterior walls. The top of the wine cellar, which was the concrete floor of the front porch, was built with a pour-in-place insulated concrete floor system. The goal was to leverage the cool ground temperature in order to make a stable wine preservation environment.

Theoretically, the combination of wine cellar materials with the superior insulation of the surrounding walls made sense. There was no insulation under the concrete cellar floor to take advantage of the constant temperature of the surrounding ground, or about fifty-six degrees Fahrenheit. This wine cellar was also equipped with a lighted switch outside the room to indicate if the lights were left on. Why? The room was so well insulated in fact that if the lights were left on too long, the room temperature would rise into the eighties and compromise the stored wine.

The room worked perfectly during the fall, winter, and spring months, and it had seemed that the theory of how the room would perform was spot on. That assumption would take a serious turn as the summer progressed and mold started to form along the floor of the wine cellar.

This mold growth baffled the homeowner, the designer, and me. I began considering the following factors that could possibly have an effect on this situation:

- There was a two inch foam barrier between the floor of the wine cellar and the basement floor. This foam barrier was installed because the team thought that there would be thermal transfer in the floor.

- The exterior walls of the basement were made of the same materials as the wine cellar walls. In those exterior walls of the basement, there were a number of windows that faced south. Some of the windows had awnings over them to provide shade in the basement, and some did not. This caused the basement to reach temperatures above seventy degrees Fahrenheit.

- There were two doors that were installed into the wine cellar area. The long room that the wine cellar was in was divided by a wall. There was an area for storing wine in bottles and an area to make wine. The doors used to enter both of these areas were interior doors like what was used in all the other rooms of the house. Under the door was a gap of about one inch.

As we considered all the factors that were involved with the mold generation in the wine cellar, one factor stood out: the gap under the un-insulated interior door. While the team spent a fair amount of time working out the way the room was going to be built and how the wine cellar would perform, we overlooked one very important issue. The mold that was growing along the bottom of the drywall, near the floor, was most intense around the entry door and faded out the farther it was away from that door. I went into the wine cellar on a summer day to inspect the mold and I immediately noticed how chilling the effect was on my arms once I entered the wine cellar. The wine cellar was fifty-six degrees and outside the door the temperature was a balmy seventy-four degrees and the air felt humid. When I was in the wine cellar, I turned out the lights. It was then that I realized what was happening. I could see the daylight of the basement coming in under the crack in the door and then realized what was causing the mold to grow in the wine cellar.

Social Media Callout Box

(Post the sentence below to your social media account.)

The heat from the interior of the home constantly is trying to move towards the colder outside temperatures.

Heat will always move towards a cooler area through conduction, convection or radiation. This is the same thing that occurs in a house during the cold months. The heat from the interior of the home constantly is trying to move towards the colder outside temperatures. That is why the insulating properties of the exterior envelope of the home is so important. This same phenomenon was occurring in the wine cellar. The warmer, more humid air of the basement family room was being pulled under the door and through the gap at the bottom of the door. The farther the warm air made it into the wine cellar, the cooler it got, thus the thinning to non-existent layer of mold farther from the door opening. The bottom of the drywall nearest to the floor was ground temperature and when the warm air passed over the cooler surface, condensation formed much like on the outside of a glass of ice water on a warm day. This condensation moistened the drywall and created a favorable environment for the growth of mold.

When this house was built, there was not as much information about the science of building, so I did most of my figuring right on the job. I researched the science of the problem and was able to determine how the mold was forming. The steps that the team found that corrected the problem was to remove the mold and treat the areas that molded. We then painted the drywall with paint that repelled mold and fungus. A weather strip was placed on the bottom of the door and fresh and return air vents were installed and connected to the house's air exchange system. This corrected the problem. This is a good example of how opposing forces work against each other to create a bad situation, and why combining technologies needs to be thoroughly researched before you start.

Know what you want?

So how do you actually determine which technologies you want to combine to create a hybrid house? I do this by giving a list of questions to the homeowner:

- What do you like about your existing home?

- What don't you like about your current home?
- What environmental hopes do you have for your new home?
- How many people will be living in the new home?
- What features do you have now that you absolutely need in your new home?
- What are your current heating, cooling, and electrical costs?
- Does anyone who will be living in the new house have respiratory problems? If so, what ailment do they have? (i.e. asthma)
- What is your budget for the new home?

Questions like these can really help zero in on the client's needs and help a homeowner to clearly define their needs. The market that is building green homes during a recession is quite specific with their needs. They are looking for someone who understands their needs and is willing to work with them on price to achieve their ultimate goal, building a home that is environmentally friendly.

Here's how it works for me. I like to meet face-to-face with the homeowner, which is what I did with a new client recently. When the homeowners answered their door, I peered over their shoulders to see every feature in their existing home. I wanted to see what level of custom work that the homeowners were expecting of us. The homeowners and I shook hands and we made our way to the kitchen.

As the homeowners and I talked about what was going to be part of the new house, I recall changing the conversation to a very important topic. I asked the homeowners "What don't you like about this house?" This question changed the conversation drastically as the homeowners both went on and on about the problems with their existing home. Knowing what your clients don't like can help a builder narrow down the things that the homeowners like.

I picked up on the "hot buttons" of the homeowners: a wet basement, cold bonus room, and poor energy efficiency in the home. Based on this and other concerns mentioned by the homeowners, I was able to work with them and their designer to create the best house for their needs and budget. The house that was ultimately approved to be built combined a number of technologies that have been discussed in this book. Here's what we came up with:

The first most important thing that the homeowners really wanted was a home that didn't look like a box. They wanted a home that had multiple angles and lots of windows in-order to take advantage of the incredible southern exposure to the sun for passive solar. This design alone immediately dictated what the main floor exterior shell would be made of. The homeowners originally wanted a home that was made of ICFs from the footings to the roof, but the size and position of the windows prevented the use of ICF—a wall needs at least six inches of concrete between each window to ensure proper bearing.

As it stood, the second choice for the exterior shell actually helped bring the home into the budget range that the homeowners wanted to spend on their project. Because the home design was not favorable for the use of ICFs on the main floor, the home was designed for Structural Insulated Panels (SIPs) on the exterior walls of the main floor. Using SIPs would still allow the house to achieve the energy efficiency that the homeowners wanted and also the SIPs would work much like the ICFs and provide great comfort inside the home; comfort that is free from drafts, cold spots, and loud noises from outdoors.

Being that we had used SIPs before on a project, we could show these homeowners examples of how the product looked, how the SIPs would work with the design and how efficient the SIPs made the overall house. Once the homeowners saw that the builder had experience using SIPs, they then were willing to use SIPs instead of ICFs for the exterior envelope of the house.

The multiple angles on this house also presented another issue: insulating the roof system. Houses with multiple angles on its interior and exterior walls always end up having a "chopped up roof" as the industry calls it. A chopped up roof is a roof system with multiple angles, valleys, peaks, hips, and gables. Because the roof system is so chopped it can make that area difficult to insulate properly because of how the roof systems are connected to each other. The attic area can be even more difficult to insulate when a bonus room is added to the roof system.

In this particular example, the homeowner wanted a bonus room for herself that was to be located in the attic area of the house. She currently had a bonus room for herself in the attic area of the house they lived in, but she mentioned that it was extremely cold during the cold months and extremely hot during the hot months. She mentioned that she would be very happy if she could be in her bonus room and not have to wear any heavy clothing during the cold months and that she could tolerate the heat during the warm months if she needed to, to have her new bonus room.

By listening to the homeowner and having her tell me all about what she did not like about her current bonus room, I was able to learn what we needed to accomplish with that area. We needed to create a bonus area for the homeowner that had the ability to maintain a certain comfortable temperature, and also, to have the ability to adjust the comfort level in that area. This can be a difficult task to do in a bonus area of a house.

Knowing that the roof system was "chopped up," and knowing that the bonus area in the attic space of a house can be very difficult to make comfortable to use the area for more than storage, the builder looked to his insulating contractor for help. Being that we had experience in insulating areas in houses like this before, I was looking to confirm my thoughts with the insulator to make sure that I was not over looking any options that would help to make this bonus area efficient.

The biggest problem with insulating chopped up roof systems is thermal bridging, or heat-transferring through a material. During cold weather, the warm air from the attic of a house can pass through any un-insulated wood members of the roof system. Many executive style homes have this problem, because it is nearly impossible to insulate certain parts of the roof system.

> **Social Media Callout Box**
> *(Post the sentence below to your social media account.)*
>
> **The biggest problem with insulating chopped up roof systems is thermal bridging.**

The roof system that is part of this example had an incredible amount of wood framing and wood trusses and would be nearly impossible to insulate conventionally. The insulation contractor and I met at the house during construction and determined that spraying open cell spray foam to the bottom side of the roof deck and around framing members was the best method of insulating this roof system. We learned on other houses that we worked on together that we would have a problem with icicles and heat loss if we didn't insulate this way.

In essence, we created a thermos. When the house was completed, this thermos turned out to be incredibly efficient. The bonus area that the homeowner wanted in her new home performed perfectly! Without setting the thermostat that was dedicated to that area of the house, the temperature of her bonus room was always within four degrees Fahrenheit of the entire house, including the basement; on any day of the year. I would never have known how important that area of the house was unless I had asked the homeowners for information. Because the issue of comfort in the bonus room was discussed before the design phase of the house, the homeowners approved the increased cost of insulation without a problem.

The bonus room of this house and the exterior envelope are just two examples of many concerns that a builder and homeowner has for the project they are undertaking. When a project team discusses a project before they begin construction, they can discover ideas before the bidding process and that helps make the budget process go smoother. Change orders come from ideas on the job site and often times occur and make a project go over budget. For the building team to work most efficiently, the builder should ask questions and offer advice towards the answers to those questions. The homeowners should listen to their builder and look to their experience to help keep the project moving efficiently.

Combining technologies to create a hybrid house will indeed give you the best of all worlds. In my opinion, the best value in building an energy efficient, hybrid house with nice amenities is to use ICFs for the basement, SIPs for all exterior walls, and trusses for the roof system. We have tried using SIPs for roof systems a few times and the

Social Media Callout Box
(Post the sentence below to your social media account.)

Combining technologies to create a hybrid house will indeed give you the best of all worlds.

equipment and manpower to set most SIP roofs is just too expensive to stay on budget. The most energy efficient and budget friendly way to build a roof system is by using trusses. Using spray foam in the roof system for insulation and around the band boards of the house is a great compliment to the tightness of the SIP walls and ICF basement. If you combine these technologies, your project cost will be more than a traditional stick framed house with poor insulation and less than a house made of ICFs.

But in the end, you will be pleased with the energy savings and comfort of this type of hybrid.

10 HEALTHY HEATING AND COOLING

As we discussed before, the best way to ensure energy efficiency in a house is to make it as "tight" as possible. That is, through proper insulation and sound building methods, let as little outside air get into the house as possible. But the question always comes up: can a house be too tight? In theory no, but in practical terms, yes. Here's why.

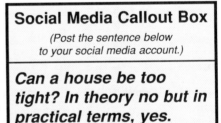

Social Media Callout Box
(Post the sentence below to your social media account.)

Can a house be too tight? In theory no but in practical terms, yes.

A house that is too air tight can cause everything from poor indoor air quality, mold, and inefficient furnaces. In this chapter I will discuss the issue of air tightness and explore mechanical ventilation systems that will show how a home can be air tight and still "breathe." I will also explain heating and cooling systems (HVAC) and how the exterior shell of the home can determine the correct HVAC system for a given house.

Good air, bad air

Once I got a call from a naturopathic doctor who told me that one of her clients was having health problems related to mold and fungus. The doctor knew I had experience in indoor air quality issues and since this woman lived in an earth-bermed house she thought I might have some answers.

When I went to the house to meet with the owners, the first

thing I noticed when I walked inside was how hot and humid it was in the house. The other earth-bermed houses that I had been in before were cooler than this house and less humid. As we talked, I learned that the wife had become so sick and nauseous that she could hardly function, often missing work. Her husband recently started to get ill after never having been sick before in his entire life. Something was obviously wrong inside the home.

From experience I know that earth-bermed houses like this were designed to heat and cool the house by having a furnace blow air over pea stones that were in the crawl space. During the cold months, the pea stone would hold the heat that was blown across it and in the warm months, the pea stone would hold the cool ground temperature which would then help to cool the house once air was blown over it. These systems had only one return air, which was located high above the family room.

When I went down into the crawl space to look around, I noticed the plastic that was covering the wood foundation and pea gravel showed signs of standing water, leaving an orange sticky residue. This stuff was everywhere, even on all of the PVC drain pipes. As I made my way back to the northwest corner of the house, which is directly below the room that seemed to have the most mold—what they called the 'mold room— I noticed condensation on the backside of the plastic that was stapled over the insulation. I cut the plastic to examine the insulation and found it all to be wet and found the treated wood foundation to be wet as well. The entire northwest corner for ten feet in each direction was wet and smelled terribly of mildew.

The house was extremely air tight and the furnace would blow air over the pea stone that would then circulate back through the living space of the home and go back into the furnace. Because the house was so tight there was no fresh air introduced into this house, so the air quality of the home was poor because the furnace would just keep circulating the same air through a minimal filter which would not take out humidity that was in the air from the damp crawl space.

My theory is that the homeowners were getting sick because the air that they were breathing was constantly being drawn over the orange sticky stuff in the crawl space. One insurance adjuster thought the orange substance was arsenic from the treated lumber. The crawlspace had held water every time it rained because the back patio had settled and was now sloped back towards the house. The air would circulate over the flooded crawlspace and the home-owners would breathe and live in that contaminated environment.

This is why it's so important to make sure you have a proper air exchange system in a tight house—it's vitally important to your health! This house was built very tight but was never given a prop-er air exchange system. It became what is called in the industry a "sick house"— a house with poor ventilation that has a buildup of mold, mildew, VOC's and other toxic compounds.

Air exchange

Proper air exchange inside a home is determined by an energy audit. I suggest that if you think that you need an air exchanger in your house, that you call a qualified energy audit service. Air exchange inside the home is best done by powered air exchangers although there are passive means that are mostly done by home-owners looking to use less energy

An air exchanger does what the name implies, exchanges the stale air in the house with fresh air from the outside of the house. The two readily available types of air exchangers on the market today are the Heat Recovery Ventilator (HRV) and the Energy Recovery Ventilators (ERV). An HRV is the most common form of an air exchanger and transfers the heat of the inside air to the fresh air that is coming in from outside. This is done before the air is exchanged. HRVs are used mostly in cold climates as a way of reducing heating costs. We have used HRVs in a few of our houses and they work very well. I have seen them combined into a forced air system where the return air of the home passed through the HRV before it reaches the furnace to be reheated.

An ERV works almost the same way as an HRV, but there is a difference. That difference is, that in an ERV, the incoming air is passed over the outgoing air and this process can actually work to pull the moisture out of the incoming air. This means that you do not introduce humid, muggy air into your home which is one of the problems that happens when you open your windows on a muggy day. I prefer to use ERVs in the house that we build for clients, as I feel that it is a better fit for the climate that we have in the Midwest. An ERV will be more effective in a house during all four seasons that the Midwest encounters.

It is not that difficult to make your own air exchanger. I have used inline fans and PVC pipe to exchange air in the underground homes that we have built. There is math that you can do to determine how many of these fans you need to properly ventilate a living space. In some areas, building codes require that air be exchanged inside a home at a certain rate. Consult your local building official if you have any questions. I have learned that the most important issue to address in hybrid houses is indoor air quality—make sure you hire a heating and cooling contractor that has a good understanding of air exchange in a house.

Options for heating and cooling

Your goal in choosing the right heating and cooling system for an environmentally-friendly home is efficiency. In other words, you will want a system that uses the least amount of commercial energy yet still keeps the home comfortable. The most common systems used in building energy efficient homes are radiant heat, forced air, and then combinations of either of those systems with "geothermal." Geothermal is a term used to describe any system that obtains its energy from the earth—we'll describe this in greater detail later in this chapter. Most heating and cooling companies have computer programs that can estimate yearly energy usage of these heating and cooling systems, taking into account the type of construction and how "tight" the house is.

Most people are familiar with forced air heating and cooling because it is the most widely used in all types of home construction. In its basic form it is a furnace with a blower that "forces" air over a heat source and then through the house via duct work. An air conditioning unit provides a cold air source allowing the blower to circulate cool air throughout the house.

Radiant heat is probably one of the oldest sources of heat for homes—early homes used fireplaces to not only cook but to "radiate" heat throughout the log cabin. For our purposes, radiant heat refers to a heat source often embedded in a concrete floor so that the heat radiates through the house.

All of these—along with variations of geothermal heating—can provide a comfortable environment in a home, but one size doesn't fit all needs. For example, I had a client who wanted me to build an SIP house for him with radiant heat because he wanted the house to be heated evenly. He had experience drafts and cold spots in his current home and felt that radiant heat would solve that problem.

I knew that the radiant heat system he wanted would add significantly to the cost of the house. The house that we built was so air tight, that once I reviewed the efficiency of each heating system, I discovered that the best system for that house was a conventional forced air system. What I have found in my work with energy efficient houses is in a tight, non-drafty house, forced air heat will feel as even as radiant heat in a drafty house.

For the longest time, heating and cooling contractors have lived by the rule of thumb that you put in a larger furnace than what the house needs so that it will run more efficiently. This idea works well in houses that are drafty and not insulated well. The extra power of the larger furnace comes in handy in cold winter months when things get cold inside the house. This rule of thumb does not apply in tight, well insulated houses. The heating and cooling contractor can use a computer program to determine which size heating and cooling system is appropriate for the house it is going into. By figuring the perfect complimenting heating and cooling system for a house, you can save money on the heating and cooling system, and on your energy costs.

On another occasion, we built a house out of ICFs that had spray foam for attic insulation, and stained concrete floors on the main level and in the basement. The house was set up for passive solar and was a similar design to a house we had built before that was very energy efficient. The homeowners wanted radiant heat, so we installed pex tubing and poured them into the concrete floors. But then the homeowners also wanted to add a geothermal system. I advised against it because I didn't think the additional $14,000 dollars was worth it. The homeowner won the debate and we installed the geothermal system.

After a winter in the home, the homeowner called me and said,

"The house warms up into the 70's during the day and never goes below 68 at night. The geo thermal system hardly ever runs." I wanted to say "I told you so," but I didn't. But I knew the exterior envelope of this house and its passive solar design would have been sufficient as the primary heating source of this home. The concrete floors were a great thermal mass and held the heat of the sun for most of the night. The floor would be cool in the warmer months and this helped to keep the house cool.

As this green economy grows, buzz words get created which get people interested in products or ideas. Geothermal is a perfect example of this because many people have heard that geothermal heating and cooling systems are a must if one is building a green home. Although geothermal has some advantages, it doesn't make much sense to install such an expensive system in a home that

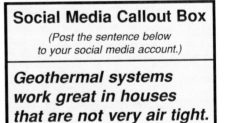

Social Media Callout Box
(Post the sentence below to your social media account.)

Geothermal systems work great in houses that are not very air tight.

was built to be highly efficient. Geothermal systems work great in houses that are not very air tight. They pay for themselves much quicker in those houses versus houses that are more air tight and energy efficient.

Still, geothermal systems will gain in popularity, so let's take a closer look at how they work. Two systems are used in home construction: closed loop and open loop systems. cooling systems work. There are basically two types of geothermal systems, closed loop and open loop.

Closed loop systems are just that—they incorporate a long tube that is buried underground which has an antifreeze mixture pumped through it. The hose is buried in a series of loops, and these loops help to transfer heat from the home into the ground during the warm months. During the cold months, the antifreeze mixture circulates through the loops in the ground and preheats the mixtures to ground temperature which the geothermal unit then takes the heat out of to heat the home. A reaction occurs in the geothermal unit that creates heat and this is how the system heats the house during the cold months. These closed loop systems can cost more than the open loop systems because of the cost of excavation for the underground loops.

In colder climates, a closed-loop geothermal system does not work as well once the outside air temperature gets at or below twenty eight degrees Fahrenheit. In the Midwest, we can go several days if not weeks with temperature below that mark, so I do not recommend installing these systems as the primary heating and cooling source. Once I asked for a bid from a company to install one of these systems, and the company making the bid insisted that we also include a back-up heating system. We obviously didn't install the system.

Open loop systems, also known as "pump and dump" systems, are used more widely than the closed loop system and in most cases it's because of the cost. Open loop systems pull ground water out of

---

Social Media Callout Box

(Post the sentence below to your social media account.)

It is not uncommon for the open loop geothermal system to discharge 500,000 gallons of water per year.

---

a well, and the water is discharged back onto the ground or into a pond after the heat is pulled out of the ground water. Open loop systems discharge an incredible amount of water, which comes out of the discharge line at 31 degrees. In larger homes, it is not uncommon for the open loop geothermal system to discharge 500,000 gallons of water per year. This makes an open loop system nearly impossible to use in areas where there is not a pond to discharge the water into, the ground water is not clean enough for the unit, and/or there is not a significant amount of ground water below the building site.

Information is your friend

Heating, cooling, and air exchange is a science. If the heating and cooling contractor doesn't have load calculation software, or know what it is, then pick another heating and cooling contractor. Load calculation software can help you confirm that your house is getting the best system to work the science of that house. If you were to use a green building program such as The United States Green Building Council's LEED for Homes program, you would be required to have the printed reports available for review by the program rater. Simply ask your heating and cooling contractor to include their calculations with their estimate. Most heating and cooling contractors have this software, as the market demands it.

I know that some of this is confusing, and mentioning some of the problems I've encountered could deter you from building a tight house. Heating, cooling, and air exchange inside of a house is as important as any other part of the system. If you spend more money on insulation thinking that it will help reduce your heating and cooling costs, you need to understand that there is more to the equation than just insulating a house properly. Once you make a house air tight, you must then consider how the house is going to perform.

But there's plenty of help for you. In addition to doing your own research on the wonderful resource called the internet, more and more heating contractors are gaining experience in selecting and installing systems that will not only heat and cool your house efficiently, but do it in a way that's good for your health.

A green house doesn't have to be a sick house.

11 RENEWABLE ENERGY

One of the hottest topics in the country for the last several years has been renewable energy. Renewable energy, also known as alternative energy, includes wind generators, photovoltaic solar electric systems, solar hot water systems, and passive solar design. Renewable energy has gained in popularity over the past few years and is beginning to show up on new homes all over the country. Let's take a closer look at the various forms of renewable energy.

Energy from the wind

Wind generators date back to 1,000 B.C., where they were used to grind grain and move water. Throughout history, wind generation has been used to move ships, pump water, and now, power homes. There are two types of wind generators, horizontal axis and vertical axis. The horizontal axis wind generators are normally on a pole and have blades that look a lot like the propellers on an airplane. All of the commercial wind generators that you hear about on a daily basis in the news are horizontal axis wind generators. The majority of residential wind generators available and used today are horizontal wind generators.

The vertical axis wind generator is the original form of a wind generator and is becoming more widely available for residential use. The vertical shaft wind generator was used originally to grind grain and help ships to sail across oceans. The vertical shaft wind generator produces its power where the wind generator shaft enters the base of the wind generator. For grinding grain in ancient times, sails would turn the vertical shaft and the resulting energy would rotate a stone on a kind of table that would grind grain into a powder.

Both versions of wind generators do make a small noise when spinning; as the wind speed increases, so does the sound the unit makes. This wind created noise on residential wind generators has been likened to the sound of wind blowing through the branches of trees, but more realistically, it sounds like a small whining noise from the motor of the wind generator and a sort of whispering sound as the blades cut through the air.

There are several options when looking to buy a wind generator to provide energy for your home. The first step is to test the site for sustained wind speeds. In other words, will you have enough wind where you live to adequately power a wind generator? Not every site is a good site for wind generation, even if you think it is always windy at the site. The best way to do this is to rent an anemometer, or wind gauge, placed as high as your plans for the wind generator. There are many services available that will rent out an anemometer and pole to test wind, but the costs can be high for this service. An alternative is to install a home weather station and monitoring the wind at your site. Generally, you should have wind speeds that average at least nine miles per hour over sustained periods of time.

Wind maps for your state can be found at www.windpoweringamerica.gov, but the problem with using wind maps to determine if a site is in a high wind area is that the wind measurements are taken at a height higher than what most local zoning laws will allow. A 50 meter wind map measures wind speeds at a height of about 164 feet, while most residential zoning only allows a 35 foot tower height on the site. Knowing the average sustained wind speed on your site is the key to selecting the correct wind generator for your site

The average sustained wind speed on a particular site is the only effective way to know for sure if wind generation will work on that site. Once the average sustained wind speed has been determined, it is time to select a wind generator. The electrical load on the house is also important to know, because this information will help a homeowner select a properly sized wind generator for their home. In most cases, budget will ultimately determine which wind generator a homeowner will select.

Let's take a look at three common examples of wind generators. For these examples, we will assume that the site has an average sustained wind speed of nine mph, and local zoning will only allow a thirty-five foot high wind generator (measured to the tip of the highest reaching blade).

Example A.

This wind generator is a horizontal axis wind generator and is widely used in residential settings throughout the world because it is nice looking and produces electricity very efficiently at the right wind speeds. This unit is a Skystream model made by Southwest Wind Power, http://www.windenergy.com/products/skystream. This unit costs $18,000, and the price includes the wind generator, mounting pole, and installation. In the right conditions, this unit will produce about 3,100 kilowatt hours (kWh) of power per year, which is enough energy to provide an average 2,700 square foot house with about half of its daily energy consumption (assuming the house is energy efficient).

This unit, at the height mentioned, starts spinning and producing electricity at wind speeds of eight mph, but doesn't reach its full energy production potential until wind speeds reach twenty-nine mph. Average sustained wind speeds of thirteen to eighteen mph are ideal for this unit and will produce the amount of energy listed above fairly consistently.

Example B.

This wind generator is a vertical axis and is readily available and very popular in residential applications. This unit costs about $10,000 installed and can produce approximately 1,800 kWh per year of power if the sustained winds are at least 11mph. This unit will produce about a quarter of the power needed to run a 2,700 square foot house (assuming the house is energy efficient). This unit starts spinning and producing energy at eight-and-a-half mph and creates power most efficiently at wind speeds of twenty-four mph. Areas with an average sustained wind speed of twelve mph would be ideal for this unit. Wide open farm fields or along highways could be a good fit for these units if the wind speeds are what the unit requires to operate. This unit would not work efficiently for our example, because the sustained wind speed of the example site is only nine mph, thus making this unit inefficient.

Example C.

This wind generator resembles a horizontal axis wind generator but actually, produces its electricity at the tips of the blades, making this unit extremely efficient. This wind generator costs around $6,000 installed and can produce around 1,700 kWh per year at sustained wind speeds of nine mph. This unit starts spinning and producing energy at wind speeds of two mph. This unit will produce about twenty percent of the power needed to run a 2,700 square foot house (assuming the house is energy efficient). This unit is designed to work in most situations and would be a great fit for our example house. In fact, two units would be a compliment to an energy efficient home and the purchase would not push the project over budget.

Will a wind generator work for you? Ninety percent of America has average sustained wind speeds of less than nine miles per hour. It is important to remember that wind generators will not work in many locations around the country because of trees and low wind speeds. There are other renewable energy options available that will be discussed shortly, so if wind does not work, maybe one of these other technologies will. Federal tax credits exist for wind generator purchases and are normally thirty percent of the total cost with no cap on the amount that can be credited.

Wind generators can cause quite a stir with neighbors and zoning officials. Before installing a wind generator, be sure to check your local zoning for height and set back restrictions. It can be a good idea to discuss the wind generator with immediate neighbors to prevent future problems

Social Media Callout Box
(Post the sentence below to your social media account.)

Ninety percent of America has average sustained wind speeds of less than nine miles per hour.

once the wind generator is installed. Never assume that your neighbors will be able to "just deal with it," because they have rights as well when it comes to site paths and property line encroachment. Deed restrictions can also prevent a wind generator from being legally installed on a site.

A separate building permit is required for a wind generator because of the footing the wind generator requires. Be proactive on the areas mentioned above to avoid any issues once the wind generator is installed. Typically, wind generators are required to be grid tied in order to work. The wind generator needs to recognize that there is electricity in the home, which means if the power is out from a storm (when it's normally very windy), the wind generator will not spin and will not produce electricity. See diagram below (http://www.windenergy.com/residential/utility-connected-homes):

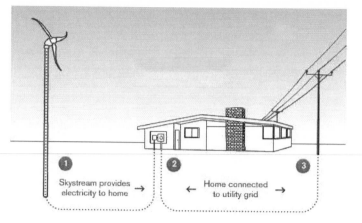

Energy from the sun

Photovoltaic (PV) solar panels produce electricity by converting the sun's energy to electricity. There are several brands of PV panels on the market today with different degrees of efficiency, and some work better in certain situations. Factors affecting their effectiveness include cloud cover, mounting availability, direction to the sun, and budget. A PV system, or PV array as it is known in the industry, needs a good southern exposure to the sun to work efficiently. The panels of the PV system must be at the appropriate angle to the sun for the system to function at its maximum potential. Most PV solar panels must be at an angle of at least thirty-three degrees, or an 8/12 pitch, to work most efficiently. This puts the PV solar panels at a perfect angle to the sun and also allows snow to fall off the panels after a snow storm. A lesser angle can be used but only with the PV solar panels that are made to work efficiently at these angles.

There are three basic types of construction of PV solar panels, with all of these types of construction using silicon in their construction. The first type of construction is monocrystalline cells, which are cut from a single crystal of silicon. They are basically a slice of crystal. This makes the slices of silicon very smooth in texture noticeably thick. Monocrystalline cells are the most efficient of the three cells but also the most expensive cell to produce. They are completely rigid and must be mounted in a rigid frame for protection.

The second type of construction is the polycrystalline (or multicrystalline) cell, which is made from a slice cut from a block of silicon. Whereas monocrystalline cells are from a single crystal, these cells consist of a large number of crystals. This gives them a speckled reflective appearance and a noticeably thick appearance. Photovoltaic solar panels made from these types of cells are slightly less efficient than the monocrystalline cells models and also less expensive than monocrystalline cells. They also need to be mounted in a rigid frame.

Finally, amorphous cells are manufactured by placing a thin film of amorphous (non crystalline) silicon onto a wide range of surfaces. These create the least efficient type of photovoltaic solar panels but also the cheapest. Due to the amorphous nature of the thin layer, it is flexible, and if manufactured on a flexible surface, the whole photovoltaic solar panel can be flexible. One problem with amorphous cells, however, is that their power output reduces over time, particularly during the first few months, after which time they are basically stable. The quoted output of an amorphous panel should be that produced after this initial period. United Solar Ovonics out of Greenville, Michigan, has been producing this type of PV solar panel and marketing it as a thin film PV product that can be installed over metal roofing.

The biggest question about solar energy has to do with location: will it work where I live? Does the sun shine enough for me to harness energy to power my home? Obviously, if you live in a state like Arizona or Florida, the answer is, "probably." But some states experience several consecutive days of cloud cover, making it difficult to harvest energy from the sun.

Social Media Callout Box
(Post the sentence below to your social media account.)

The biggest question about solar energy has to do with location: will it work where I live?

For the purposes of illustration, let's examine a test house that is located in southern Michigan. This house has approximately 2,700 finished square feet and has three bedrooms. The occupants are a retired couple with one son left living in the home. The house has a geothermal radiant heat system and is set up passive solar in design. This house is built entirely of ICFs on all the exterior walls and is extremely energy efficient. The house was designed to face south, sits in a big field, and has 330 square feet of roof space available for PV solar panels. The rule of thumb for PV solar systems is that 1,000 watts (1 kW) will require 100 square feet of PV solar panels. Given that the house had 330 square feet of useable roof space for PV solar panels, the house was figured for a 3,300 watt (3.3 kW) system. All of these facts are relevant when deciding what PV solar system to put on a house. Other considerations should be, annual days of sunshine, annual snowfall totals, and how open and free of shade the site is.

The next step would be to determine what the electricity usage is in the house to see if the 3.3 kW system would produce enough energy to make the investment worth it. As mentioned above, this home was built to use very little energy, with the geothermal heating unit being the largest electrical draw. Because the house was built out of ICFs and was designed to have the sun heat the home through passive solar, then the geothermal unit would not be running as much as a normal home, thus lowering the amount of electricity the geothermal unit needed to run each twenty-four hour period. For this home, the site is not suitable for a wind generator because of a line of trees that blocks some of the wind to the site, so PV solar was the right choice for this home.

But, does solar work in Michigan? The answer is yes. Over a given year, this home's PV solar array produces nearly 3,500 kWh of electricity, which equates to about sixty percent of the total energy needs for the home. The homeowner has been open with the results of his system, because he wants to educate others about solar energy in Michigan. He states that he has to be realistic with his expectations of the system and realizes that when it rains and snows, the panels are going to produce minimal to no electricity. His family adjusts their energy usage on the days when the PV system is not producing as much electricity. This system is connected to the grid and has no battery storage system, which could be added at some point to this system if the homeowner so chose.

This homeowner has been able to give incredible insight into PV solar production in Michigan and makes it very clear that success in his PV system was the result of science and not anyone's opinion. That should be your only criteria when considering solar energy: what do the scientific facts say?

Here are a few more details about the PV system on the home in southern Michigan that might apply to your own situation: snow does build up on the panels and takes a day or two to fall off the panels. Panels can be cleaned off, but this can be dangerous and can damage the PV panel. The homeowner recommends letting nature takes its course, as the snow always melts away once the sun comes out. Sharp manufactured the PV panels for this example house, and they are so efficient, that the PV panels produce electricity on rainy days and by moonlight! This 3.3 kWh PV solar system cost $28,000, but qualified for a federal tax credit, which was thirty percent of the total cost of the system with no cap. The tax credit added up to $8,400 and made the system have a net cost of $19,600!

Not all areas of the country are ideal for PV solar systems, and through science, one can tell if an investment in PV is a good idea or not. As mentioned above, houses in Michigan and other Midwest locations can benefit from PV solar arrays, and it takes an understanding homeowner with realistic expectations to realize the full potential of the system.

When it snows, the panels get covered up if they are mounted to a roof with a pitch of 8/12 and less. PV panels that are mounted on brackets or tracking units that are not on a house can shed snow faster, because they typically are mounted at a greater angle. Production of electricity through PV panels is greatest in the summer months when there are less clouds, and the sun is in better line with the PV panels.

The federal tax credits and different incentive programs that are available from time to time through the utility companies are starting to make the payback on PV solar system worth buying. Because of this, expect to see more homes being equipped with PV solar arrays which ultimately increase the value of the home and reduces the homes demand for energy bought from the utilities.

Hot water from the sun

Solar hot water systems are one of the most economical, usable renewable energy systems available today. Solar hot water systems are basic in design; each style of solar hot water panel has a panel or tube that an antifreeze mixture flows through. This mixture is heated and is pumped through a closed loop into a storage tank. The water in the tank heats up as the solar heated mixture flows through a heat exchanger in the storage tank. This solar heated hot water is used for domestic hot water in the home, and the solar hot water system can be integrated into a radiant heat system with the right configuration.

See illustration below (www.solarenergyfactsblog.com):

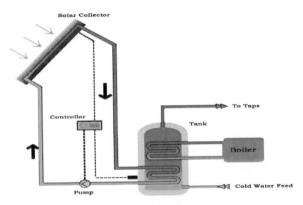

There are two main types of solar hot water panels: flat collector panels and evacuated tube collectors.

Flat panel solar hot water collectors. Flat panel collectors follow the basic design of putting a closed loop tube of liquid in an oven-like box. Most of the piping inside a flat plate collector is very narrow, sometimes the inside diameters of the tubing is not larger than a 1/8 inch. The flat plate collector is more efficient in most instances because of the narrow piping and enclosed panel system. The flat panel collector is more efficient on sunny days than on cloudy days. The flat plate collector's efficiency is directly related to its position to the sun, making this style of collector efficient for only a certain part of the day. Snow can build up on flat panel collectors and decrease their efficiency drastically.

Evacuated tube collectors. Evacuated tube collectors use glass tubes and vacuum to heat the antifreeze mixture in the closed loop system. Evacuated tube collectors are extremely more efficient in cloudy and cool conditions than the flat panel collectors. Evacuated tube collectors are able to collect more of the sun's rays than a flat panel collector, because the round tubes are always perpendicular to the suns ray. Another advantage that the evacuated tube collector has over the flat panel collector is that the gaps between the tubes actually help to prevent snow build up on the collectors.

Solar hot water systems are a great value. As mentioned briefly above, there are two major styles of solar hot water systems. Is one better than another? To answer this, science can help.

> **Social Media Callout Box**
>
> *(Post the sentence below to your social media account.)*
>
> ***Solar hot water systems are a great value.***

Consider this example: If Customer A lives in an area with more cloudy days than sunny days, the evacuated tube design would be a more efficient system. Customer A most likely lives in an area with high annual snowfall, and the evacuated tube design can help shed that snow to help the collectors work more efficiently.

The evacuated tube design heats water more efficiently than flat panel collectors on cloudy days, so if a homeowner is like Customer A and has similar conditions on the site where the solar hot water system is to be installed, than an evacuated tube solar hot water system is most likely the best fit. Flat panel collectors can be better adapted to wall mounting and architectural pleasing designs.

If Customer B lives in a sunny area that sees more sunny days than cloudy days, and their site is positioned towards the sun, then a flat panel collector system would be more efficient in this setting. Research shows that the efficiency of the flat panel collector sharply decreases during the cold, cloudy months in Michigan. Customer B would be very happy with the hot water production of her system from March until November in Michigan; she would be less than thrilled at the hot water production during the remaining months of the year.

Both styles of solar hot water heating mentioned above could qualify for a federal tax credit of thirty percent of the total system cost with no cap on the credit given (when the grants are available). Most solar hot water systems with two collectors cost around $8,000 installed. The thirty percent tax credit would be $2,400, making the average net system cost with two panels an affordable $5,600!

Passive solar design

Passive solar is the art of heating and cooling a home by positioning the house on the building site and using roof overhangs to harness or block the sun's rays. Passive solar design is the one thing on a home that has virtually no added cost, but can save the homeowner incredible amounts of money on heating and cooling.

Here is a diagram to show you how passive solar works. (www.ecohomeduluth.com)

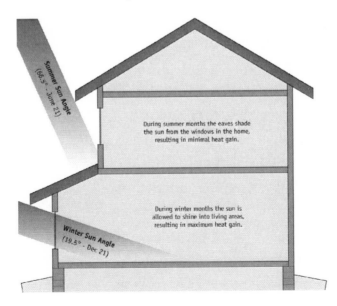

Summer Sun Angle (66.5° - June 21)

During summer months the eaves shade the sun from the windows in the home, resulting in minimal heat gain.

During winter months the sun is allowed to shine into living areas, resulting in maximum heat gain.

Winter Sun Angle (19.5° - Dec 21)

In Michigan, passive solar works very well. The optimal roof overhang size in Michigan is thirty-six inches. This overhang size will put a shadow line six inches below the bottom of a house's windows during the hottest months of the year. The house is shaded by the overhangs during the hot months, which keeps the house cool. An advantage of the thirty-six inch overhang, besides the passive solar qualities, are the "heals" that are required on these trusses for such a large overhang. This heal is known as an energy heal and gives you superior insulation depth in the area where it is most needed, where the exterior walls meet the trusses. The energy heal also allows for maximum air flow in a ventilated attic system.

In Michigan, positioning the living areas of the house five degrees to the southeast will ensure most efficient passive solar qualities. The sub-contractor that sets the footings is responsible for positioning the house correctly. The builder or homeowner should be on site when the footings are being set. Using a compass and a transit is the easiest way to position these footings correctly. Set the transit so that true north on the compass is "0" on the transit. If the transit is turned 180 degrees, the transit will be pointed to the true south. If the transit was turned to 175 degrees off of true north, which is set to "0" on the transit, the footings and house will be positioned five degrees to the southeast.

I tried to explain how to sight a house to the concrete company that was installing our footings on this one particular house. I even went out to the jobsite to explain the process. With that said, you can imagine my concern when the homeowner called me the night before the footings were to be poured and told me he thought the house wasn't sited properly and that the footings were off. This call came as I was in the middle of eating, I remember asking for a to go box and ate my dinner in the truck as I raced two hours away to check out the footings

When I got to the jobsite, I could tell right away, that the house was not sited properly. The portion of the house that we needed to face towards the sun was facing ninety degrees in the wrong direction. It just so happens that the house needed to be parallel with the road that ran in front of the house and that was the reference line that the concrete company needed to use to site the house. I remember one of the young concrete guys saying, "We have to redo all of the footing form boards, what's so important about this house facing that way?" Since I heard him say that, I pulled him and the other guys over to the south side of the foundation hole and showed them why we had to have the house facing the way we needed it to face. When the house was built and that crew came back to pour the driveway slab, I brought them into the house and they got to see firsthand how well the house heated with just the sunshine that poured in through the windows. That same young concrete guy was in awe and said "Wow, that's why we moved the footings."

In the following pictures, the wall with all of the windows is the passive solar wall of the house. This back wall of the house was sighted using the transit techniques mentioned above. The first picture shows the home under construction on the longest day of the year, June 21. Notice where the shadow line is, it is below the bottom of the window!

The windows of this house were designed to passively ventilate the home. The awning units of these windows are on top of the windows to increase air. The combination of the shaded house from the overhangs and the passive ventilation means that this house does not require air conditioning in the summer time. The house very rarely gets above seventy degrees, even on the hottest days of the year, and it costs nothing to keep the house cool! Notice the shadow!

Passive solar designed homes heat up inside the home during the colder months of the year, because the sun drops in the sky, and the overhangs no longer shade the house from the sun. Using ICFs or SIPs helps the home to hold this free heat longer and keep the heating system from running in the home. Documented proof of homes heating up to 73 degrees Fahrenheit in February, when it is 10 degrees outside but sunny, exists in nearly every corner of the Midwest.

The house in southern Michigan mentioned earlier is one such house. This house heats up to 73 degrees during a sunny winter day, and the house holds the 73 degrees until well after the sun sets and eventually, drops below 70 degrees around 1am. The homeowners have their thermostats set at 68 degrees Fahrenheit and because of this, the heating system in the house runs a few times between 3 am and 8 am, until the sun starts shining into the home. This is free renewable heat! Simply by designing a site specific house and placing that house properly on the building site.

Passive solar is by far the most affordable form of renewable energy. If a builder or homeowner designs and sights the home properly, the house can be heated by the sun on sunny days during the colder months and cooled by its overhangs during the warm months when the sun is higher in the sky. This is free heating and cooling for a home. Passive solar will save homeowners money and makes the home more valuable. If the budget did not allow many options on a home, and one was trying to make it greener, money should be spent on the low additional costs that a passive solar home requires to build. These additional costs are stronger trusses, more glass in the windows. There are no other renewable energy options available that has the payback that passive solar has.

To recap, remember that the most important thing to consider before you spend money on a renewable energy system is that you need to be aware of the amount of energy that you are currently using. Look for ways to reduce the energy that you currently use. When we build someone a new house, we always know what their energy use habits are. I ask the homeowners to fill out an energy use plan which tells us how to set their new house up so that they use less energy. Once we know how the house will perform, then we add renewable energy systems to the house to compliment the entire system.

I have never believed in buying things because it is what everyone is talking about. Renewable energy was that same way. Now, renewable energy has dropped in price and increased in efficiency and makes a lot of sense.

EPILOGUE

I hope you have come to the conclusion that you can "go green" and save money, because you can. But aside from saving money, building an energy efficient home is the right thing to do if you value this wonderful planet we were given. Yes, sometimes it gets a little complicated trying to figure out just what type of construction you will use, or what materials are best suited for your location. And initially, you may have to shell out a little more money to have a green home built. But imagine how you will feel when you know that the house you are living in is having minimal impact on the environment.

As the cost of fuel increases—and we know it will—more and more builders will learn how to build energy efficient homes. Suppliers will create even better construction materials, often from recycled products. Consumer will have even greater choices, both in terms of design and type of construction.

I'm proud to be a pioneer in this movement and will continue finding better ways to build environmentally friendly homes. It has been my passion for as long as I can remember, and I hope that reading this book has ignited the same desire in you. If we all work together, we can ensure that our children and grandchildren will be able to enjoy the same wonderful planet that we do.